Praise for *Why This Jubilee?*

James Howell took me to the most familiar Advent/Christmas hymns and songs—ones I have sung for years—and made me pay attention in a whole new way. "The cattle are lowing" is a new image in my mind after reading how Saint Francis created the first manger scene. I want to sing with the angels, worship with the shepherds, bow before my Lord Jesus, and follow him this Advent in a deeper way. Read this book. Your imagination will be stirred, your heart moved, your feet led in new ways!

—Rev. Leighton Ford
Presbyterian minister, author, mentor,
and president, Leighton Ford Ministries

Music has the power to immediately evoke a time, a place, and a memory even beyond the text's meaning. Howell takes us on a delightful journey into the heart, history, and meaning of Christmas carols in a way that deepens our experience of them in unexpected and unforgettable ways. We fall in love with them and with the mystery of the season all over again.

—Dr. Marcia McFee
Creator and Visionary, Worship Design Studio

There is something alluring, even magical, when through music "God imparts to human hearts" the joy of Christmas, of Christ. James Howell is a wonderfully gifted writer and a theolog... i-
cian as well. I can think of no ... s

for us all to help us ponder more "the hopes and fears of all the years." Highly recommended.

—Dr. Ben Witherington III
Amos Professor of NT for Doctoral Studies,
Asbury Theological Seminary

Why This Jubilee?

ADVENT REFLECTIONS ON SONGS OF THE SEASON

JAMES C. HOWELL

UPPER
ROOM BOOKS®
NASHVILLE

Cover design: Marc Whitaker / MTWDesign
Interior design and typesetting: Kristin Goble / PerfecType

Library of Congress Cataloging-in-Publication Data

Howell, James C., 1955–
  Why this jubilee? : Advent reflections on songs of the season / James C. Howell.
    pages cm
  ISBN 978-0-8358-1495-9 (print)—ISBN 978-0-8358-1527-7 (mobi)—ISBN 978-0-8358-1496-6 (epub)
1. Advent—Meditations. I. Title.
 BV40.H697 2015
 242'.332—dc23
                                        2015001161
Printed in the United States of America

To Jimmy, Ellen, John-Palmer, Kevin,
Jenni, Dongho, Patrick, Catherine, Jean, Glenda,
and quite a few other musicians in gratitude for our friendship
and for the privilege of leading so many wonderful
Advent and Christmas Eve services together.

Contents

Third Week of Advent: The Mother

Fourth Week of Advent: The Child

Introduction

*J*esus loves Christmas carols even more than I do. A few years ago, I sat next to Kevin Siers, who since has won a Pulitzer Prize for his clever and provocative political cartoons, at a dinner party. It took place during Advent, and Siers shared with me that his favorite phrase to ponder among all Christmas carols is "the hopes and fears of all the years are met in thee tonight." I realized I had cheerfully sung carols all my life but hadn't done much pondering.

Since that night, I've slowed down a bit and discovered hidden riches in words and phrases I'd never taken the time to ponder. I deeply admire carols, and they have helped me grow close to the Lord whose coming we celebrate and for whom we long. When by God's grace I get to heaven, I'll look for Phillips Brooks, Franz Gruber, Christina G. Rossetti, Charles Wesley, and Isaac Watts. I'll tell them how much their compositions have meant to me. Perhaps I'll even find the unknown composers of "O Come, O Come, Emmanuel," "Away in a Manger," and "The First Noel" and express my awe and appreciation for their work. These composers noticed something about the Bible's narrative; they understood nuances I missed. And their poetic eloquence provides us windows through which we can watch for the coming of the Lord. They have made me stammer before the beauty of the Lord, then graced me with the music so I might articulate my awe and wonder. I hope to thank them and ask if we could go caroling together.

This is a book of reflections for the days of Advent. We will explore the characters in the Bible stories and the theological themes that color our thoughts as we lean toward Christmas. The phrases from familiar carols will yield their secrets and serve as companions on our journey of waiting, repenting, expecting, and finally joyfully celebrating. We will ponder "Mild he lays his glory by," "How still we see thee lie," and "No crying he makes." We will ask "Why lies he in such mean estate?" and "Shepherds, why this jubilee?" "How silently the wondrous gift is giv'n" and "Let ev'ry heart prepare him room" might just alter our routine during Advent and bring us peace.

By Heart

Let's reflect on the simple fact that we have a special genre of songs known as *carols*. There isn't a narrow style or instrumentation that makes a carol a carol—and carols are beloved by fans of classical, rock, country, and hip hop music. Carols evoke a sense of home, warmth in the cold, light on even the longest of nights. Everyone seems to know the words to "Silent Night" or "Joy to the World" or "O Little Town of Bethlehem." We can all sing along—in fact, it's hard not to sing along! Never is music more unifying, never do we feel so deeply than when we are part of something larger than ourselves. It pleases the Lord Jesus when we sing of his coming with carols we know by heart. *By heart.* We know the words without looking, and those words resonate in the parts of us that dream, love, and yearn.

It is no accident that we own albums exclusively devoted to music of this season. We don't have summer CDs or March Madness MP3s. Yet we celebrate the wonder of Advent, the glory of Christmas with song—a season so luminous, so eloquent, so tender that a melody is required, harmonies emerge, and even the sourest Scrooges may surprise themselves by opening their mouths to join in the song.

There are Scrooges during Advent, and I've been one of them. Maybe you have too. And with good reason: We can sing our hearts out, but a nagging hollowness follows us even in the midst of well-festooned Christmas frivolity. If we've ever grumbled, "Bah, humbug," we're only paying attention to our hearts and the disjointed, vapid, and just plain tragic state of the world.

At the turn of the twentieth century, on a desolate, cold day in December, Thomas Hardy considered the bleakness of the world as he wrote "The Darkling Thrush," for he felt "fervourless," "unaware" of such a thing as hope. Understandably, he concluded there was "so little cause for carolings."

We can "do" Christmas. But when we ponder the news, the culture, maybe our own anxieties and griefs we struggle to hide, or strained relationships, we shudder. God seems as far away as the North Pole. Jesus feels very "once upon a time." The carols we recall are pretty, but nostalgia only carries us so far.

As we will see, the carols themselves remind us of the cause for caroling—without denying the darkness of our world. The Lord doesn't ask us to pretend it's not dark or that we're not surrounded by ugliness. Our most cherished carols are not totally buoyant and sunny. Their words embrace the darkness and the light, the sorrow and the joy. Advent perches on the border between light and darkness, shining and shadow. Shadow isn't total darkness. We suffer much loss, but we persevere. We feel sad, but we need not despair. Life is there—as is death—always. Light shines brightest when it breaks out of the shadows.

In defiance of whatever bleakness the world offers, we still have cause to sing. Our plea to "come, O come, Emmanuel" to us who "mourn in lonely exile here" is answered: "For Christ is born of Mary." Wearied by a world of crassness and violence, we peek behind the veil and recall that "he rules the world with truth and grace." It's true: "The hopes and fears of all the years are met in thee tonight."

So "come, let us adore him." We are not alone. God does not dwell in remote isolation. God comes down—God has come and will come down—for God cannot bear to be apart from us, even those of us who forget about God or aren't trying to get close to God. The love that made the universe—you, me, and all of creation—is approaching. With God's help and others singing along by heart, we can raise our voices in song.

The Place

The whole notion of Advent can seem a bit ethereal, hard to touch, smell, or envision until we remember that December is a month stitched tightly to our souls in particular places—sacred places, even. For me, I recall richly textured Christmases from my childhood in the small town of Oakboro, North Carolina, where Mama and Papa Howell made the celebration a grand festival of love and joy for me and their other grandchildren.

When the Lord finally came, he came to Bethlehem—not the sort of place a sensible God would choose as the pivot on which all history would turn. And yet there it is: Bethlehem, the unlikely place, with nothing to boast about were it not for the birth of a child. There it is on the other side of the world: Bethlehem, a focal point of political turmoil, its massive West Bank Wall an ambivalent witness to a secured peace that is the ironic absence of peace. In every place, wherever we are from, in all of our Bethlehems, we mourn "in lonely exile here." We cry out for the Christ child.

How Still We See Thee Lie

$\mathcal{I}$ find the question "What is your favorite Christmas carol?" to be virtually unanswerable. It depends on which one I'm singing at the moment. It depends on who's with me and where I am. Some carols boom—I sing them at the top of my lungs. "Joy to the world!" Volume is required and inevitable.

Other carols require a whisper. They evoke a hush, a placid quietness even as they make their gentle sounds. "Silent Night," "Away in a Manger," "Lo, How a Rose E'er Blooming"—not many decibels on those.

How Silently the Wondrous Gift Is Giv'n

After visiting Jesus' birthplace in 1865, Phillips Brooks penned his great carol "O Little Town of Bethlehem," and it is a treasury of quietness: "How still we see thee lie," "The silent stars go by," and then "How silently, how silently the wondrous gift is giv'n." *Silence*—a stranger we may have met but have since forgotten, neglected, or avoided. Perhaps the greatest gift we could give ourselves and one another would be to befriend silence, to block out some time, to be still, to quiet our hearts and minds, to hear the coming Lord whisper, "Be still, and know that I am God" (Ps. 46:10).

A medieval tradition suggests that when Jesus was born a hush fell over all the earth for a full hour; even the dogs did not bark. We have grown accustomed to so much racket! Maybe we prefer the noise; perhaps we fear that silence might blow through our hollow souls like a chill wind. But the wind might prove to be the Spirit of God—and God is a lover of silence.

Imagine the inevitable, brief silence that fills a room after someone receives the perfect gift. Sitting near the tree, she picks up a box, yanks off the ribbon, tears away the paper, lifts the lid, removes some tissue paper, and her eyes open wide—and in the silence we wait, we wonder. She hoists her new prize and only then speaks: "It's a. . . ." Well, it doesn't really matter what it is, does it? It is love wrapped in a box, a feeble attempt to say, "I love you. You matter."

In that little town of Bethlehem, lying so still, silent stars lingering over sleeping mortals, the wondrous gift of God's own self was given. Some despair saying, "I can't hear God saying anything to me." But silence is God's language. The silence is God's wish for peace in our souls and in the world.

If we could jump on a plane and fly to Bethlehem, would we encounter a still night? The tourists will have gone to bed, and the shopkeepers are resting up for another day of peddling souvenirs made of olive wood. But a quiet night in Bethlehem is only possible because of an uneasy truce. A massive wall knifes through the little town of Bethlehem; we see lots of barbed wire and soldiers ready to pounce on potential peace-breakers. Graffiti on the wall pleads for peace, a silent but unmistakable protest—against security? Who wouldn't want security? Is it really security when guards point searchlights and guns at anything that moves?

Might Advent be a time to protest all our security and safety measures? We lock things up, but doesn't this only lock up our souls in fear? Could it be that we cannot experience peace and joy until we get quiet? In politically tense places, what if the decision-makers grew quiet and listened to the sounds mothers make when they've lost sons or daughters through war and violence? Could we quietly build trust instead of walls? In our daily lives, could we learn the beauty of silence? Could we listen more than we talk? Could we take the risk of extending compassion to others instead of always playing it safe?

Let Every Heart Prepare Him Room

On Christmas Eve, right after we raise our candles in the darkness and sing "Silent Night," the church lights blaze back and we sing "Joy to the World!"—including the intriguing plea, "Let every heart prepare him room." One year I remember muttering, "Too late now."

Yet here we are in the first week of Advent. We still have a chance to prepare room for the coming Christ child. Perhaps we should start today—only four weeks of shopping left! Only four weeks to get ready for Jesus left! We complain about the excesses of Christmas, but if there is excess in December, it only reminds us that we suffer from an excess of stuff, busyness, and silliness all year long. My schedule is jammed full—and not just in December. My soul overflows with anxiety, impulses, cravings, and wounds. I'm booked—which ironically is why I feel so empty.

When Jesus knocks on my door, he hears me holler, "Hang on a minute!" While he waits, does his mind drift to the story his mother told him about the inn in Bethlehem having no vacancy? What Jesus wants for Christmas is a vacancy, an opening, some room. He can't be crammed into my heart if I keep everything I've ever accumulated. I have to do some letting go; I have to begin my spring cleaning in the early days of winter. For me to say yes to Jesus, I will have to say no to a few (or many) other things. Is Jesus interested in my ability? Doesn't he crave instead my availability? Can my praying be listening more than talking? Dare I pray, "Speak, Lord, your servant is listening"?

We want to listen, but we delay. Frederick Buechner imagines the Bethlehem innkeeper looking back years later on that fateful night, detailing how hard it is to run an inn, how there are a million details to attend to, and how he wasn't lying—there really was no room in his inn. In fact, the innkeeper was not there for the birth of the child. "But this I do know. . . . All your life long, you wait for your own true love to come—we all of us do—our destiny, our joy, our heart's desire. . . . When he came, I missed him. Pray for me."[1]

Is there room in our hearts, in our lives, for Jesus to come? If we have no joy, is it because we have no room for joy? God has built a room inside each one of us, a little chapel, an inn designed for Jesus to come and reside within us. But hasn't it become overgrown with weeds, cluttered with rubbish? The room in me seems too shabby for the splendid Lord to enter.

But no room is too shabby. Jesus was born in a frigid stall where the cattle were housed. You have the room. Take a long look at the pile of baubles and busyness and decide this is the year to "let every heart prepare him room." Pull down the cobwebs; wield the heavy-duty vacuum. Don't miss your true love, your heart's desire.

DAY 2

Yet in Thy Dark Streets Shineth

*W*hat time of day was Jesus born? Carols unanimously agree it was in the middle of the night. "It came upon the midnight clear," "The stars in the sky look down where he lay," "Silent night . . . wondrous star, lend thy light." "The First Noel" happened "on a cold winter's night." Why might God choose a place of darkness? Maybe the rationale is found in the less familiar "Christ Is the World's Light," which lauds Christ for entering the darkness to become our brother. An increasingly popular hymn sings "I want to walk as a child of the light . . . The star of my life is Jesus. In him there is no darkness at all." Darkness serves as far more than a symbol. Who's afraid of the dark? Children in their beds—and grownups in their beds. Things go "bump" in the night, and I shiver when my mind plays mean-spirited games on me in the dark. We reach for comforts, either medications or alcohol, to help us sleep.

God showing up in the dark is of considerable comfort to us. In Psalm 56:8, a struggling insomniac trusts in God: "You have kept count of my tossings; put my tears in your bottle."

That's a prayer for Advent! And I am reminded of a night when my daughter was sick with a fever. My wife and I took turns going into her room in response to her cries. The last time I went in I asked, "Sweetheart, do you need anything?" She said, "Yes, Daddy. I need you in here."

We need God in the dark—Emmanuel, God with us. How fitting that carols are situated in the dark. How fitting that the longest night of the year falls during Advent. The nights grow longer and longer throughout December, but then just a couple of days before Christmas there's a barely detectable turn. After the winter solstice, sunrise is just a fraction earlier, sunset a few moments later. The light is growing.

Back to Bethlehem, where "the silent stars go by," where "in thy dark streets shineth the everlasting light." Just how dark was Bethlehem? Today Bethlehem can be quite dark—then glaringly bright with police spotlights scanning this troubled zone of tensions between Israelis and Palestinians. When Jesus was born, Bethlehem would have been dark indeed, with only a few pottery lamps glowing, each casting light no more than a few dozen feet. The most noticeable light would have been the starry canopy, which is almost completely obliterated in our cities due to the flood of artificial light. Back in 1865 when Phillips Brooks visited and was inspired to write his beloved carol, Bethlehem was still just as dark as it was when Jesus was born.

The artificial, purchased, generated light is our darkness. We flip switches, pay our electric bills, even buy long-lasting light-bulbs. But these lights are all our doing. In ancient Bethlehem, light was a gift, light was precious, light was never taken for granted or mastered. The gentle light of the night sky was not merely pretty; it evoked the very goodness and beauty of God.

The Everlasting Light

One of the darkest Advents ever had to be the one of 1941. Winston Churchill had come to visit with President Franklin Roosevelt, two political giants trying to devise a plan to thwart Nazi and Japanese aggression and rescue Western civilization. Noticing the decorative lights on houses around America, the British prime minister caught in their slight flickering a glimpse of hope in the dreary darkness of the world plunged into war. Then on Christmas morning he and Roosevelt went to church, and Churchill heard (for the first time!) "O Little Town of Bethlehem." He was deeply moved.

In December, our streets are unusually bright from the glittering of twinkle lights hanging from trees, candled wreaths perched in windows, and garlands of lights strung from roofs and doors. Perhaps as we take in the lights, we will witness God's love and feel the presence of hope in even the darkest days of history, or of our own lives—and see more deeply the "everlasting light" that "in thy dark streets shineth."

The most casual churchgoers, the diffident who've given up on church, even the least spiritual people in every town—everyone seems to be stirred by the little lights that adorn our neighborhoods in the dark during the Christmas season. In the quiet streets of a Sunday morning in most American cities, a respectable though dwindling number of people drive to church buildings to attend worship services. But in the dark streets of December, there is cause for celebration, and everyone feels it. The cynics, the unchurched, the "nones," the agnostics, and those spiritual persons who eschew organized religion—they string lights in their homes with abandon. Is it merely because of custom? Or is there even some dim awareness, the unrealized but unquenchable hope that maybe, in this one story of a child, a mother, the beasts in the manger, a chorus ringing across the dark sky, God might somehow be palpably manifest in it all?

Dickens penned these hopeful words for Scrooge's nephew: "Christmas is the only time I know of . . . when men and women seem by one consent to open their shut-up hearts freely, and to think of people below them as if they really were fellow-passengers to the grave, and not another race of creatures bound on other journeys."[2] Who's really below us anyway? Who went lower, became more humble, and bore more poverty than our Lord Jesus?

The little town of Bethlehem was graced with a shimmering light no one could fully comprehend. Rembrandt's "The Adoration of the Shepherds" portrays the infant Jesus as luminous, glowing like a lantern, illuminating the faces of everyone gathered around him. Perhaps when our dark streets shineth we will see not just a culture run amok or neighbors who annoy us or strangers who puzzle us but fellow passengers who also inhabit God's good world.

DAY 3

God Imparts to Human Hearts

*L*et's continue with Phillips Brooks's marvelous carol, "O Little Town of Bethlehem." The third stanza suggests that God's "wondrous gift is given." Is the gift the Christ child? The next phrase requires some reflection: "So God imparts to human hearts the blessings of his heaven." We can speak of the numerous blessings from God: the firm ground under our feet, food that grows from the earth, sunshine, faces and bodies that smile and embrace, even resources we might use to make life good. But what are these "blessings of his heaven"? They are given "to human hearts"—not to our bank accounts, to our accumulated pile of stuff, or even to human hands. God is quite involved in what is tangible, but God's deepest passion is for the heart. The heart is that marvelous, elusive part of us that loves, longs, hurts, connives, wonders, dreams, and believes. God's blessings include things, but heavenly blessings are deeper, richer, and more lasting than what we eat or drink or buy or wrap or wear for a few seasons. Blessings are love, promises kept, tender affection, hope in God's future, the belief that we are not alone.

When we think about the blessings that indeed are from heaven, we pray with confidence, "Your will be done, on earth as it is in heaven" (Matt. 6:10). Without knowing what heaven will look like (and we may safely assume heaven will exceed our grandest expectations), Jesus invites us to ask that a perfect, wonderful reality begin to take place now, on earth. So ask for peace, love, and certainly hope—and not just for ourselves and for those we love but for everyone. If heaven has no war, no prejudice, no hunger but an overflow of compassion, mercy, joy, and love, then our agenda for today and the rest of our lives is set. As Martin Luther King Jr. reminded us, if there are long robes in heaven and milk and honey flowing sumptuously, then everyone down here should have clothes and three square meals a day.[3]

Advent invites us to shun Christmas-y notions of asking God for blessings like well-behaved children, a great job, good health, and a nice house. God came to the poor; God blesses all people. Since Jesus said, "Blessed are the meek" (Matt. 5:5), and since the world despises or pities meekness, I like that the carol sings, "Meek souls will receive him." Not proud souls, vapid souls, or even achievement-oriented souls but meek souls, humble, open, grateful souls. To such, the "dear Christ enters in."

God helps not just those who ask but all God's children. Advent is the season when Christ comes to those who resist, ignore, and ridicule him. If God has boxed up some gifts for us this year, we may open them to find not neat goodies we've always wanted but harsher realities we might prefer to leave unopened.

The saints who lived closest to God have opened their divine gifts and discovered that following Jesus can and does leave you marginalized, ostracized, wounded, in danger, and even dead. God has given me what I never asked for. For much of it I am grateful; from the rest I try to learn and grow.

What gifts do we desire from God? Our Christmas lists will seem trivial compared to the riches God wants for us. God's job isn't to grant our big wishes. God shows us something higher, far beyond what we could wish for on our own.

"The blessings of his heaven" are still more. A great cloud of witnesses resides in heaven. The attitudes, faith, and heroism of St. Francis, my grandmother, Mother Teresa, and a holy host of others inspire, cajole, and lure us this Advent. With them one day, we will bask in the most delightful blessing of his heaven: the marvelous, unmediated, face-to-face presence of our Lord.

O Come to Us, Abide with Us

So many of the songs we sing at Christmas ask the Lord to *come*: "O come, O come, Emmanuel," "Come, thou long-expected Jesus," and the final plea of "O Little Town of Bethlehem," "O come to us, abide with us." God already came. How can God come when God is everywhere? The word *come* implies God might be gone and needs to return. If anyone needs to return, it would be us back toward God. Yet in the Bible, it is the Lord who comes. Ours is to wait. We sense somewhere deep in the marrow of our being that the Lord isn't here but will come again. Perhaps this deep part of us feels empty; perhaps we don't know how to fill the emptiness. As we look out our windows into the darkness, we plead desperately, "O come to us!"

The peculiarity of Christianity is that we know God is everywhere all the time, and yet we still celebrate the mystery of God embarking on the impossible: coming to us. God came not as a thunderstorm or as an armed invasion but as one of us, a baby. God didn't come to a sumptuous palace but to a ramshackle, cold manger in the middle of nowhere, to a bunch of nobodies.

How good of God to love us enough to become one with our very life and to show us God's tender heart by having a heart like ours. How would we have had any clue otherwise? We would always have thought God was invisible, omnipotent, infinite—everywhere. But I find I don't need God to be everywhere; I need God to be here. I don't need an infinite, ineffable God. I need a God with a heart who loves, a God who will come to us and abide with us.

The saddest words I remember from childhood holidays came in my grandparents' living room when all the presents were unwrapped, the cleanup nearly done. My dad tapped me on the shoulder and said, "Son, let's go. Christmas is over." But we know better. We sing not only "O come to us" but also "abide with us." Linger a bit longer after the presents and food when we're back in our routines, at work or school—"abide with us." After all, Jesus' name is *Emmanuel*, meaning "God with us." Some of John Wesley's last words before his death were "The best of all is, God is with us."

Sleigh Ride

When I was a boy, my family had an album (the old vinyl 33 rpm kind) of Christmas music. My favorite song was "Sleigh Ride," performed by the Boston Pops with the percussion section capturing the crack of the whip and the clopping of horse hooves, a trumpet mimicking the horse's whinny. This cheerful Christmas song is about going for a ride, the long lost custom from the days when families and friends spent a lazy afternoon going nowhere in particular and in no hurry. And in a sleigh!—a fantasy for a boy like me growing up in the deep South. I find the warm affection of the lyrics alluring since they evoke images of snuggling, holding hands, and calling out to friends.

At many weddings, I read what was read at my own wedding, Colossians 3:12-17, which offers superb counsel on how to be friends, family, neighbors, or just human beings on this planet: "With gratitude in your hearts sing psalms, hymns, and spiritual songs to God" (v. 16). There is a crooner, a pop diva, a karaoke fool inside each of us. But it's no fun to sing alone in December. When the family wants to turn on TV, when friends are trying to think up something to do, or when the office party gets a bit stodgy, be the one to say, "Hey, let's sing!" Maybe something simple like "Away in a Manger" or, if it's safer, something secular, like "Jingle Bells."

God is pleased when we ride, when we lay aside our productivity for a spell and simply see and feel the out-of-doors, the stuff God made. God is also pleased when we lift our voices in song. Some healing happens in the soul. If the Bible is any indicator, most of eternity will be spent singing with others.

Mary and Joseph went for a long ride together. Actually, they probably walked. If they brought a donkey along, it was to carry their bags and provisions. What an arduous journey! The terrain is rocky, steep in places, the weather moody. Predators, bandits, and fierce elements lurked. Today an obstetrician would not advise traveling ninety miles on foot and sleeping outside with no shelter. Mary and Joseph probably sang to stiffen their courage and bolster their spirits. Pilgrims habitually sang psalms—"How lovely is your dwelling place . . . My soul longs, indeed it faints for the courts of the LORD" (Ps. 84:1-2). "One thing I asked . . . to behold the beauty of the LORD" (Ps. 27:4). "Sing to the LORD, all the earth. . . . The LORD is king! . . . Let the heavens be glad, and let the earth rejoice . . . for he is coming" (Ps. 96:1, 10-11, 13)—lyrics echoed in several modern carols.

This was Mary's second journey while pregnant; first she had ventured to Judea to visit her kinswoman Elizabeth, and she sang then too! "My soul magnifies the Lord, and my spirit rejoices in God my Savior" (Luke 1:46-47). What I'd give to hear her voice and the melody.

Lots of people took to the roads because of Caesar's census that first Advent—hence the full inn the couple found on arrival in Bethlehem. Around campfires at night along their way, some may have spoken of Ruth, their ancestor, who had made a long, sorrowful journey there from Moab with her grieving mother-in-law, Naomi. The magi may have already been on their way from the exotic East. Caesar Augustus and King Herod probably had troops on the move to ensure security. Even the angels came down from heaven, as did God, in the traveling revelation of the Divine as Emmanuel, God with us, God making a very long journey to be one with us.

Have Yourself a Merry Little Christmas

Like Mary and Joseph, many of us take to the roads to gather with friends or family in old hometowns or new cities as Christmas draws near. How intriguing. At Thanksgiving and Christmas, we get together—not as we usually do with friends or neighbors of our own choosing, but with family, the unchosen ones. These get-togethers are, for some, treasured moments of immense joy. For others, the days are strained, awkward, and maybe a bit painful. If extended families were summoned by a census to make journeys home, Mary and Joseph had to be united with some siblings, cousins, aunts, and uncles. How did that go for them? Did they sing? Was there whispering among those who did the math on Mary's large belly? Did she have to urge Joseph to remain calm?

There is some holy virtue when we stick with those people we're stuck with. We practice this art during the holidays. Old feelings—both the warm, fuzzy ones and the gut-wrenching ones—bubble up to the surface, and we feel small again, vulnerable, cozy or cramped, hurt or whole.

We sing, "O what fun it is to ride . . . laughing all the way." Maybe. Maybe we laugh, or perhaps we cry. We'll gather, yes, but this will be the first Christmas without Grandpa. We'll gather, indeed, but how will I explain the absence of my wife? We'll gather, but will Mom recognize any of us? We'll gather, but a brother will be arrogant and prickly as always.

As we make room in our schedules and spaces for the people we're stuck with, how do we simultaneously make room for Christ? These challenging relationships may well be some kind of training in holiness. We are in relationships we cannot escape. We know the worst about one another, but we have to deal with it. So we learn mercy and humility. We realize Christ's presence in the faces of these people God has given us as kin.

And these unchosen ones also play roles in our futures; of that we can be certain. God has ordained it to be this way for us. This assured future settles a few issues and might help us to calm down. We really will be together—and so we might as well be patient and love as best we can. And when we do, there is room for Christ to come.

The Cattle Are Lowing

We cannot imagine manger scenes without animals making an appearance. We sing, "The cattle are lowing" and "where ox and ass are feeding." "The Friendly Beasts" even features speeches for the donkey, "shaggy and brown"; the cow, "all white and red"; the sheep "with curly horn"; and the dove "from the rafters high."

But no one thought of such scenes until Saint Francis of Assisi. A year before his death, Saint Francis visited his friend Giovanni in Greccio. He asked Giovanni to erect history's first manger scene, complete with a straw crib, oxen, donkeys, and an image of the infant Jesus. The townspeople gathered on Christmas Eve bearing torches. The friars sang hymns and medieval carols. I especially try to imagine Saint Francis's voice, for on that night, overcome with emotion, he preached, and listeners said his voice sounded like the bleating of a lamb. Saint Francis picked up the infant figure and held it in his arms. Some said they thought they saw the child come to life. This little town of Greccio was transformed into Bethlehem, far away geographically but very present in spirit. Saint Francis's devotion to the humanity of Christ was tender; he understood that God was not aloof. God didn't show off with overwhelming power. God became small and vulnerable; God invites us to offer love and tenderness to others just as God offers those things to us.

On that glorious night in Greccio, Saint Francis ordered that all the animals be given a double portion of food. How odd for Saint Francis since he was famous for his fasting. That juxtaposition of fasting and feasting suggests a dimension of Advent we seldom consider. Advent can be something of a fast that ends in a festive banquet come Christmas night. We might give up something for Lent, but give up something for Advent? Choosing hunger during December? How counterintuitive! And thus rich in spiritual possibilities. And if we've fasted, how marvelous would the feast on Christmas day be? Jesus said, "Blessed are those who hunger and thirst for righteousness" (Matt. 5:6). Could this Advent be the Advent we finally intensify our hunger for God and pursue righteousness with the abandon of shoppers pressing into the malls on Christmas Eve?

One legend tells us about a wolf that had been terrorizing the town of Gubbio. Efforts by armed posses had failed to stop the beast. Saint Francis went up into the hills, found the wolf, and spoke to him. "Brother Wolf, you do much harm in this area. But I know very well that you did all this harm because there's no food in these hills." Francis made a deal: If the wolf would confess his sin and promise not to terrorize the people any longer, the people would feed the wolf every day. Saint Francis reached down, and the wolf offered his paw in return. At first the citizens of Gubbio were on their guard. But after a time, Brother Wolf came in and out of their homes at his leisure. When he died, the citizens of Gubbio wept.

Food is often the beginning of justice. Dorothy Day opened dozens of shelters for the poor, the first being her own tiny 15th Street apartment in New York. Lines formed. She served up stew in the front room. In the back room she published *The Catholic Worker*, protesting working conditions in urban America and calling a lazy church to action. Holy justice happens in simple places like the dinner table. Day explained, "My mother used to say, 'Everyone take less, and there will be room for one more.' There was always room for one more at our table."[4]

My grandparents, Mama and Papa Howell, exercised such basic hospitality when I was a little boy. There was always enough; an extra cousin or a day laborer or a passerby was always welcome. I loved Christmas in their home, and it may well be that the joyous welcome at Christmas represented a natural extension of the open table they provided year round.

Away In a Manger

It is entirely fitting that during Advent most churches (and now even secular organizations) collect food for the needy. We sing that it was in a manger where "the little Lord Jesus laid down his sweet head." A manger was, of course, a feeding trough for animals. God becomes flesh in the very place where hungry animals look to find sustenance. And this manger was situated in

Bethlehem. The Hebrew, *beth-lehem*, means "House of Bread." Where else would the Bread of Life come down?

Jesus' most provocative conversations unfolded while breaking bread with others. He miraculously multiplied bread, and there was even bread left over, exhibiting his abundant generosity. When he wanted his closest friends, the disciples, to understand what was about to happen to him, he broke a piece of bread so they could remember his immense love long after his flesh had actually been broken. The Bread that came down to the House of Bread in a trough is the Bread of Life.

If God's revealed identity is so focused on bread, maybe you should get busy feeding people who are hungry. Can you grow spiritually in food giving from one Advent to the next? Heeding Wesley's admonishment that it is better to deliver aid than to send it, you could go to and connect with someone who is hungry. Finally, drawing very close to Jesus, you could invite the hungry into your own home for a shared meal and fellowship.

Saint Francis made Greccio a new Bethlehem. That very year, Crusaders were in combat with Muslim armies, vying for control of holy places, including Bethlehem. Saint Francis was saying we do not need to fight to get to Bethlehem. Any place—even Greccio—can be Bethlehem. Any place can be the place where Jesus comes. At every tense border where there is strife, we pray "Be near me, Lord Jesus," but we also pray that Jesus be near them, the others, until that day when "they shall beat their swords into plowshares" (Isa. 2:4) and when "the wolf shall live with the lamb . . . and a little child shall lead them" (Isa. 11:6).

The Hopes and Fears of All the Years

The most thought-provoking phrase in all the carols pertaining to Bethlehem may just be in the first stanza of Phillips Brooks's "O Little Town of Bethlehem": "The hopes and fears of all the years are met in thee tonight." We are people who hope because we were created in God's image. Even in the midst of terrible circumstances, we yearn for a brighter tomorrow. And yet we still fear. All creatures get scared. But we humans are unusual; our fear sits with us, even if there's nothing jumping out to frighten us in the moment. We fear failure, rejection, aging, and death. Fear fuels our anxiety.

Hope and fear seem to be antithetical, as if they emerge from opposite ends of the soul. But aren't they kin, intertwined, burgeoning out of the same place inside? Aren't they twin impulses toward a future that might annihilate us but also reward us richly?

Our hopes might be simple. I hope my turkey will emerge from the oven and be tasty. I hope I get to my church's Christmas Eve service in time to get a good seat. Then other hopes are huge and cut deeply into the soul. I hope for peace in the world or in my conflicted family. I hope my brother will make it through Christmas. And now I notice my fears are clutched very tightly around my hopes: I'm afraid he won't make it. I fear family squabbles. I'm anxious in the kitchen with a house full of guests.

At this intersection of hope and fear comes Jesus, born in Bethlehem at the crossroads of the continents, where "the hopes and fears of all the years are met." We meet Jesus at this intersection, and he meets our fears and calms them, meets our hopes and fulfills them. "O holy Child of Bethlehem, descend to us, we pray; cast out our sin and enter in, be born in us today."

Easy to sing. But can it be so simple? The fears of all the years, the fears of our lives today—we need to sort through what we fear, why and how. If I am in the street and a truck is bearing down on me, I should be afraid. There are helpful fears, but much of our fear is excessive or irrational. How riddled are we by anxiety? Politicians and advertisers play on our fears. When fear assumes the dominant place in daily life, we security-hungry people stop taking risks.

Advent is a risky business. God took the risk of assuming human flesh. The Bible's most frequently repeated commandment is "Fear not." How often does this play in the stories of the first Advent? The angel tells Joseph not to be afraid to marry Mary; Zechariah is told not to be afraid; the angel Gabriel tells

Mary not to be afraid; the angelic chorus tells the shepherds not to be afraid. Yet I find the Bible's admonition to "Fear not" only makes things worse. I was fearful, and now I feel worse by disobeying God or failing to let God calm my fears. Author Lauren Winner came up with a clever idea: give up anxiety for Lent. But that's as well nigh impossible in Advent as it is in Lent.

How do we give up anxiety unless we can replace it with something else? Here's Lauren's strategy: When anxiety would rise up, she would recite little prayers she'd learned from liturgy. "O God of peace, who taught us that in returning and rest we shall be saved, in quietness and confidence shall be our strength: by the might of your Spirit lift us up, we pray, to your presence, where we may be still and know that you are God." I printed these words on a little card and keep it in my pocket.

We need reminders. We need to keep our eyes on God. Instead of being overwhelmed by our fears, we let God's love overwhelm our fears. During Advent, to breathe in God's overwhelming, joyous life, I find I need to breathe as well. For those of us who battle anxiety, a secular therapist will advise us to breathe deeply. How biblical—God breathes life into us, Jesus breathes life into the centurion's daughter, and the resurrected Jesus breathes on his disciples. Here's what has blessed me: Throughout the day, I stop, I am still, I know that God is God. I breathe out fearful thoughts and anxieties, and I breathe in the grace of God.

Once in Royal David's City

Martin Luther King Jr., not long before he was assassinated, explained that hope was different from optimism, and while he still possessed the former, he did not cling to the latter. Optimism is the very American mood that tomorrow will be a better day; that if we do our best, all will be well come tomorrow. Hope is different. Hope depends not on us but on God. Hope can cope even if tomorrow is actually worse than today. Hope involves justice and the conviction that wrongs will be made right. Advent is a season of justice, and we can feel confident in God's work in the future because of its foundation in God's work of the past. Christ has already come after all.

God's past in Bethlehem causes us to sing, "Once in royal David's city," "Of Jesse's lineage coming," "O come, thou Key of David, come." Even one thousand years after David was king, Israel never stopped longing for another king like him. They should have longed not for a king like David but for a *boy* like David. When he was young, his heart was full of love for the Lord; armed with nothing but faith, young David courageously ventured out and toppled the gigantic warrior Goliath. But once enthroned in his palace in Jerusalem, his childlike dependence upon God shrank as his stature soared. He murdered; he seized women on a whim.

Think back to that Advent moment in David's childhood. God informs Samuel that one of Jesse's sons will be the next king of Israel. It turns out to be little David, not the big, impressive sons of Jesse! God's logic trumps once more. God uses the small, the unlikely, the ones with hearts for God. "The Lord does not see as mortals see; they look on the outward appearance, but the LORD looks on the heart" (1 Sam. 16:7).

Advent is a new way of seeing. Never gawking over the superficialities the world panders to, Advent looks deeper. How do I embrace this Advent way of seeing? Do I dare to be *seen* the way the Lord sees? The Lord looks on my heart. This notion frightens me. My heart is a tangle of darkness, mixed motives, a tug of war between noble impulses and tawdry cravings.

But the Lord keeps looking, the Lord is merciful, the Lord never stops seeking a vulnerable willingness in my heart. The facade crashes down, and I discover the love and empowering direction of God. My fears and hopes finally meet. Jesus is right there, and I am not afraid.

The Men

In a funny, memorable scene from *A Christmas Carol*, Charles Dickens imagines a caroler singing "God Rest Ye Merry Gentlemen" at the door of old Ebenezer Scrooge, who angrily seizes a ruler and chases the terrified singer away. When my denomination published a new hymnal in 1989, "God Rest Ye Merry Gentlemen" had been chased from its pages. Was it the gender issue? Or a wish to avoid social elitism—the word *gentlemen* implying class status? What is a gentleman anyhow? In another Dickens classic *Great Expectations*, old Joe beholds Pip, whom he has not seen since Pip was just a little boy, and says, "Yes, Pip, dear boy, I've made a gentleman on you!" Pip has grown and matured; he is not a wild or rambunctious youth. Isn't there something in the coming of Christ that might make us mature, even gentle?

Can we imagine singing to the men in the Bible stories of Jesus' birth, "God rest ye merry gentlemen"? Were they merry? In the original carol, there was a comma after "merry." God rest ye merry, gentlemen! We are invited to rest in a "merry" way. Rest is hard to come by for gentlemen, gentlewomen, all of us really. But there's something at the heart of Advent about God giving us rest and the merry joy of resting in God.

We turn now to an array of men who figure prominently in the narrative of the Lord's coming. From them, all of us—women, men, and children—might learn much about waiting on or missing out on this Lord's coming and the way to be merry.

DAY 1

Until the Son of God Appear

During the early days of December, the music we hear in shopping malls and on the radio is frothy, cheerful, bouncy, gleeful: "Jingle Bells," "Feliz Navidad," "Let It Snow!"—while church people dourly sing Advent hymns. And the scripture readings are even more depressing: John the Baptist, bellowing his dire warnings, "Repent, for the kingdom of heaven has come near" (Matt. 3:2), "You brood of vipers!" (Matt. 3:7), "Even now the ax is lying at the root of the trees; every tree therefore that does not bear good fruit is cut down and thrown in the fire" (Matt. 3:10). Not very Christmasy.

Theologically, Advent has been conceived as a season of repentance. Does Jesus want us to grovel or groan with guilty feelings? What is it to repent? The original languages help us a little. John the Baptist would have deployed the Hebrew-Aramaic word *shûv*, which means to make a 180° turn. You're going the wrong way! Turn around and head back toward God! A lovely image—but what would that look like for us during Advent? The Greek word the Gospel writers used that we translate as "repentance" is *metanoia*, which means a change of mind. But what would that look like during Advent?

Here's a pregnant possibility: Advent isn't about thinking different thoughts. We spend Advent thinking about someone, the One, and not just the facts about that someone but thinking about him the way a parent ponders an infant's fingers or a young lover considers his significant other, the way a grandmother in a nursing home checks her watch, eager for the grandchildren to arrive. We think about Jesus. John the Baptist did. A repentant mind focuses on Jesus and remains unattached to other things.

John the Baptist presided over the final years of the longest Advent, that centuries-long Advent that couldn't look back to the Lord's coming but only forward. His ministry was leading "captive Israel" in a song of yearning. John's birth was a marvel. Elizabeth's pregnancy? She was older than a grandmother. In what may be the Bible's most poignant, moving moment, Mary, many months pregnant, visits her cousin Elizabeth, further along in her pregnancy, and as these two holy expectant mothers converse, Elizabeth's baby gives her an especially stiff kick, as if detecting from the dark, cozy womb the presence of the One who would come and ransom captive Israel.

Mourns in Lonely Exile Here

Repent! Was John's tone of voice as loud and raspy as I've imagined? What if his voice was more plaintive, a little bit melodic, gentle, even sorrowing or sighing? If "there is therefore now no condemnation for those who are in Christ Jesus" (Rom. 8:1), then how could John denounce us in condemning tones? Advent isn't scolding. As I grow older, I have come to hear John's voice as tender and loving, with long sighs and a fair amount of sorrow.

In ancient times, Nebuchadnezzar conquered Israel and forced its people to live in exile in Babylon. Out of place, surrounded by an alien culture, the Israelites felt pressure to conform, to fit in, to squander their identity as God's holy people. They wondered, "How could we sing the LORD's song in a foreign land?" (Ps. 137:4). Enmeshed in a culture that is not of God, we too may feel restless and hollow, although we don't know why. We long for home even in our native land. Deep inside, we want to find our way back to our simple, genuine selves, back home with God. For we are captives until God sets us free.

In the meantime we find ourselves in a kind of mourning. We feel anxious; we feel something's missing no matter how much we have. Somewhere deep in our guts we feel lonely, even at a party brushing elbows with dozens of jolly folks. We stay very busy, staving off deep sorrow. And so it will be for us "until the Son of God appear." The pain and loneliness can sting more acutely at Christmas. Though the holidays can bring gladness, we may find that our joy resides next to a deep sadness, which may be why laughter can bring tears and why we are moved emotionally in this season like no other. Jesus said, "Blessed are those who mourn, for they will be comforted" (Matt. 5:4). We find our comfort in Jesus, our Emmanuel—"God with us."

Sin and Error Pining

The sinning that John the Baptist frets over isn't being naughty now and then. It is being broken deep inside. It is life in a fallen world. During December we likely will hear a soloist or choir sing "O Holy Night," which eloquently attests to our desperate need for "the dear Savior's birth": "Long lay the world in sin and error pining." Sin, old as the earth and as overgrown and festering as kudzu.

But pining? Rarely used nowadays, *pine* means "to desire," "to long," "to hanker for," the way you crave the pie your mother used to make, the way people who do not know God flit about from one amusement to another, not realizing it is God alone who can satisfy. We pine in our error and sin, hungry for a holy life, for regular personal contact with the creator of the stars and universe. Jesus came on that holy night to mend our broken lives.

And so quite hopefully on Christmas Eve we sing, "Cast out our sin, and enter in!" Cast out? We might prefer a gentle nudge! But our sin—our niggling determination to go it on our own, our crass habit of hurting others and ourselves—requires superhuman strength to overcome given the tenacity with which we cling to our old lives. We tell ourselves, *One day I'll read my Bible, volunteer, and try to be holy*. But can we really dally another year? John the Baptist, whispering to us tenderly, will prove to be our best friend this Advent.

St. Joseph's Carol

$\mathcal{N}$ot many of us have heard of "St. Joseph's Carol" or "When Joseph Went to Bethlehem" or the lullaby "Joseph Dearest, Joseph Mine." Joseph gets little attention in Christmas singing.

He's used to it. Joseph has always been relegated to the background of Christmas pageants, looking on, doing nothing much besides gazing, peering over Mary's shoulders, hanging on to the donkey's reins, his face solemn, looking a little bit sheepish, even foolish, while attention is focused on the Jesus and his mother Mary. No dramatic skills are required to play Joseph. He's just there.

We don't know much about Joseph—and the little we do know seems ridiculously inconsequential. He worked in construction; he was a laborer who worked hard for a living. Not a star. Oddly, God's highest calling might be for us to be like Joseph. He was simply there. He stuck close to Jesus, and that was enough. As the psalmist states, "For me it is good to be near God" (Ps. 73:28).

Something else on Joseph's resume: He was virtuous. Was he a titan of holiness? I see his greatest virtue as something humbler and harder: He was merciful. He does not shun Mary after she becomes pregnant. He had his rights; in those days, to be betrothed was more binding than a mere engagement today. Once betrothed, the groom assumed legal rights over the bride, and the arrangement could only be broken by a legal divorce. The law threatened the death penalty for a woman caught in adultery. We can only guess as to the gossip Joseph overheard, the chilly stares he and Mary received. But he is quiet and prayerful enough to be in sync with God's Spirit on this one, and so he refuses to pass judgment. He stays.

Maybe Joseph had been shown mercy and knew what it felt like. When Jesus is grown, he tells people who know precious little mercy, "Blessed are the merciful, for they will receive mercy" (Matt. 5:7). Jesus doesn't just talk mercy. He is abundantly merciful to people who knew no mercy at all: lepers, demoniacs, and tax collectors. Had he witnessed this in Joseph? Weren't Jesus' best parables—the prodigal son and the good samaritan—all about mercy?

Deep inside, don't we crave mercy? Don't we all need to be tender, merciful, and forgiving to others? Joseph is the namesake of a man who personified mercy: Joseph, the son of Jacob. Joseph was eminently wise, and he forgave his dastardly brothers who sold him into slavery and broke their father's heart. He saw through all their misdeeds and perceived the divine plan: "Even though you intended to do harm to me, God intended it for good" (Gen. 50:20).

How do you and I get close to Joseph, who was close to Jesus? I am adept at finding fault and zeroing in on what's wrong with others. But Jesus came so we would not judge, so we could become merciful and receive mercy ourselves. A judgmental thought rings your doorbell? Don't answer. A critical remark hangs on your lips? Stay silent. An ugly observation about somebody out there, someone you love, or even yourself, suggests itself? Take a breath, and imagine Joseph hovering lovingly next to Mary, whom he could have despised, and over Jesus, God's love bundled in the manger.

Joseph would not fit in our cynical culture very well. We are quick to doubt, swift to blame. A jaded skepticism rules our lives. We are determined never to play the fool. But Joseph believes Mary's story—and God's—and chooses to court the shame and embarrassment. He trusts. He stays.

Mary, Joseph, Lend Your Aid

Joseph can help us. Confronted by the scandalous surprise of God becoming flesh, granting every good reason to flee for the exit and be the center of attention in our own dramas, maybe this Advent we can learn what it means just to stand near the manger, to look, to wait, to stay, to trust.

In the carol "Angels We Have Heard on High," the most intriguing line in the carol, to me, is this one: "Mary, Joseph, lend your aid." God came down and became vulnerable, just a child in need of tender care. Mary and Joseph held God in the flesh, nursed, rocked, and fed him. They aided our Lord—just as every time we offer aid to the poor, the needy, the lonely, we aid our Lord. Yet the carol tantalizingly uses the word *lend*. Yes, we may use *lend* as simply giving or offering. We may say, "Lend me a hand!" But the word *lend* can also denote the act of loaning something. If we lend something, we expect it to come back to us, and in fact good lenders loan and get the investment back with interest. Mary and Joseph lend aid to Jesus, and what they get back is the King of kings, life and salvation in the one they rocked during the night. When we lend aid in Jesus' name and out of love for him, don't we receive back more than we could ever have given? Not that our bank account grows because we give to the poor. Rather, we give, we offer aid, and we are repaid with a sense of fullness, with meaning, and with feeling closer to God.

We may presume Joseph died before Jesus began his public ministry, as he is unmentioned in the Gospel stories. In Nazareth in the first century, people died at home. Surely Mary and Jesus were there by his bedside. I picture Jesus holding his father's hand, wiping his brow, and lifting his eyes in prayer. When Joseph breathed his last, Jesus saw. Each one of us hopes that, at the hour of death, someone, or a few someones we treasure, will be there to love us, to say good-bye, to shed a tear or two. We are like Joseph—but since it is Jesus who was by his bedside, and he eventually becomes the Risen One, I can be quite sure that if my loved ones aren't there when I leave this good earth, I will not really be alone at all. Standing there will be Emmanuel, "God with us."

DAY 3

King of Kings

*W*ithout thinking about it very much, we speak and sing of Jesus as royalty. "Come, thou long-expected Jesus . . . born a child and yet a King." Both "What Child Is This?" and "Hallelujah Chorus" from Handel's *Messiah* praise Jesus as "King of kings." And the fourth stanza of "O Come, O Come, Emmanuel" declares "Before thee rulers silent fall." What an audacious, absurd, easily falsifiable claim! The rulers were far from silent. They made noise! The silence was in Bethlehem, broken only by a lone baby's cry in the darkness. Once Jesus was grown, Pontius Pilate did all the talking, and Jesus was stunningly silent.

Ask anyone on the streets of Bethlehem on the day Jesus was born, "Who rules?" Trembling in nervous awe, anyone would say Herod or Augustus. Herod ruled Judea, Augustus the vast empire of which Judea was a part. The two rulers were friends, the way powerful persons are in cahoots with one another in order to cling to and expand upon their power. The story wouldn't be nearly as rich if Jesus had been born during the reign of Galba, Nerva, or Elagabalus, impotent rulers perched on their thrones during the weakest of days. Augustus was the greatest, the longest ruling, the quintessential ruler that Rome ever knew. Then Jesus came!

It was Augustus's unusual decision to conduct an empire-wide census that brought Joseph and Mary to the place Jesus was born. We think the powers do what they do because they are all-powerful. But God uses even the high and mighty, unbeknownst to them, to achieve God's purposes.

Who could be more unlike Augustus than Jesus? Augustus, it was said, came to Rome when it was made of brick and left it covered in marble. Jesus came to Bethlehem in a cow stable and left bleeding on a cross. Monuments from France to Asia to Africa boast of Augustus's achievements. When Jesus died, no triumphal arches were erected. Augustus brought peace, the famed *pax romana*, enforced by legions. Jesus, the Prince of Peace, wielded not a single weapon, save the absurdity of love. Augustus was deified by fawning officials who dubbed him "savior," and his birthday was titled "the beginning of the good news." But no one reading this book knows Augustus was born on September 23, and the real "good news" had to wait until Jesus had died and been raised.

Sometimes we forget Advent's political edge. If this Lord who is coming really is the King of kings, then the lords and kings of this earth have cause to be jittery. When Christians said, "Jesus is Lord," the clear, treasonous implication was "Caesar isn't Lord as he claims to be." Herod isn't either—and how intolerant was he of rivals? He had two of his own sons strangled to death, along with the boys of Bethlehem days after Jesus' birth.

Once Jesus was grown, he showed no interest in forming a rival government or overthrowing the government of Rome. Was Jesus a threat to the status quo? Clearly he was, and he is in every age. The ironies in our carols are profound: "He rules the world . . . and makes the nations prove the glories of his righteousness." The nations would swear they certainly were not proving the glories of Jesus' righteousness! But the nations, all of them throughout history, do bear mute witness to the glory of the living Lord. Look at the ruins of ancient Egypt or ancient Rome, the tumbled columns and crumbled palaces of Ramses, Augustus, and Herod. They prove that even the greatest human power eventually collapses. The very fact that fear drove every such emperor to surround himself with armed guards proves they were not secure.

Chains Shall He Break

Earthly kings do not bless, but they certainly do oppress. During Advent or on Christmas Eve, we may hear "O Holy Night." The final stanza is theologically intriguing: "Chains shall he break for the slave is our brother; and in his name all oppression shall cease." Citizens of Bethlehem knew too well the oppression of King Herod and his henchmen. Herod was the darling of the Roman world and one of the most prolific, impressive builders in all of antiquity. His structures and cities dazzled. But it was poor Jews, like Mary, Joseph, and Jesus' disciples, who bore the burden of excessive taxes to fund this building extravagance. Herod's tax collectors knew how to squeeze citizens for their last shekel. Imagine the scandal when Jesus actually befriended these tax collectors! And that is how he broke the chains of oppression—not by out-oppressing the oppressors but by befriending them.

Herod the Great was admired, yet so very pitiable. On his deathbed, he ordered the elite of the city to come to the hippodrome, had the gates locked behind them, and ordered that they be executed to guarantee an outpouring of grief when he himself died. The magi were lucky to get away after riskily saying to Herod's face, "Where is the child who has been born king of the Jews? For we observed his star at its rising, and have come to pay him homage" (Matt. 2:2).

Sometimes Bible readers get mixed up about which Herod was which. Herod the Great ruled when Jesus was born. But it was Herod Antipas, his son, who reigned when Jesus was crucified. There also was Herod Archelaus, Herod Philip, and not one but two Herod Agrippas in the Bible! But really, Herod, Herod, and Herod are the same guy. All were egotistical, insecure petty potentates in bed with the Romans and clueless about God.

During Advent, we glory in the humble and small. Herod felt threatened by a small baby. Once that baby was a grown man, his friends fanned out into the world and provoked riots. Paranoid authorities complained, "These people who have been turning the world upside down have come here also. . . . They are all acting contrary to the decrees of the emperor, saying that there is another king named Jesus" (Acts 17:6-7). But not just another king. The King. The King of kings. Emmanuel, before whom rulers silent fall.

Shepherds Quake

The first shepherd I saw on my first pilgrimage to the Holy Land shattered every sweet, romantic image I'd harbored. He was wearing an Elvis T-shirt, stomping around in yellow galoshes with a long switch in his hand, swatting at hapless sheep, hollering what my guide told me were expletives. We sing about milder, gentler shepherds: "Shepherds in the field abiding," "While shepherds watched their flocks by night," these "certain poor shepherds in fields as they lay." Should we pity them for being poor, exposed to the elements "on a cold winter's night"? Most shepherds were poor, humble laborers—but so were the vast majority of people living in Palestine in Jesus' time.

We see something noble tucked inside the identity of every shepherd. David had been a shepherd, and the great kings of Israel's heritage were often called shepherds of their people. Many Jews believed passionately that a great shepherd Messiah would usher in the reign of God. And if all that weren't enough, Jesus ensured that *shepherd* would become an even more magnificent title, because he, the Good Shepherd, gave his life for the sheep.

The popular carol "Silent Night" was perhaps never more powerfully sung than during World War I when German and then Allied soldiers lobbed cakes, bottles of rum, then Christmas trees at each other (instead of grenades), and then gingerly walked into No Man's Land and raised their voices together to sing "Silent Night." I wonder how those soldiers felt when they looked at each other and sang "Shepherds quake at the sight."

Is there anything that can make us quake? We have a shriveled, shrunken view of the universe, assuming everything is manageable and we are smart enough to figure out all we need to know. But for the shepherds, and for virtually all Christian worshipers until recently, there was something numinous, a mystery, an elusive power before whom you quaked. The shepherds had come face-to-face with that ominous presence of God before—in the temple in worship. God was in God's holy temple; mere mortals bowed their heads, their knees wobbled a bit, their breath taken away. Worship is an encounter with the living God. We quake. The shepherds had experienced this in the temple quite a few times.

Before the looming, mind-boggling, stupendous presence of God in God's holy place, we quake. It's all we can muster. In worship, we adore, we bow, we humbly offer a sacrifice we know is nothing to such a great God. We plead for mercy; we delight in the sheer privilege of being able to brush up against the hem of God's magnificent garment. Maybe at Christmas, when we lift our candles and remember that the shepherds quaked, we might quake and recover that lost sense of worship. The Lord is in his holy temple. The Lord came down as a baby wrapped in swaddling clothes, his garment of light and life, and we fall on our faces, blown away by the magnitude of God's presence, measured in tiny fingers and a meek cry. We sing, "Christ the Savior is born!"

Whom Shepherds Guard

The shepherds "went with haste and found Mary and Joseph, and the child lying in the manger" (Luke 2:16). We associate the lovely tune "Greensleeves" with the beloved carol "What Child Is This?" I find myself intrigued by the phrase "whom shepherds guard and angels sing." Shepherds don't sound like very good guards, do they? Lacking armor and swords, they have never been drilled in formations or in protecting against violent attackers. They lack uniforms and dignified precision, like those guards at the Vatican or Buckingham Palace. Chasing sheep around in the dark doesn't qualify you to guard a king like Jesus.

But the shepherds stood before Jesus in awe, the way we crowd around a crib that holds a sleeping child. Theirs was a guarding of faith, belief, hope, and love. Jesus asked for no protection. When armed assailants showed up, he asked God to forgive them even as they nailed his perfect, beautiful body to a piece of olive wood. Pilate was shrewd enough to hire a guarding detail to hover around Jesus' tomb. But they did not believe. They did not hold Jesus in awe like the shepherds did, and their guarding was futile, for God raised Jesus from the dead for the sake of shepherds and children and poor folks and all of us who worry a lot about security but can never finally make ourselves safe. We can only trust God with our future, which is a glorious one, if we can trust what the angels are singing.

Shepherds, Why This Jubilee?

Very few words have made the trek from the ancient Hebrew language to the English we speak today. A lovely one is *jubilee* (and its kin, *jubilant* and *jubilation*). Originally the Hebrew word signified the ram's horn, which was blown to gather the people for grand religious festivals. Leviticus calls for a year of jubilee (see Leviticus 25) every fifty years, when that horn would be blown announcing forgiveness of debts, freedom to slaves, and restoration of sold or conquered lands. We can imagine the raucous delight of such a day—well, for the poor at least. For those who had bought land, owned slaves, or were owed money, the year of jubilee may have felt sorrowful. The Bible has a peculiar bias toward the poor and needy, a "leveling" passion that all will have enough, quite apart from who deserves and who doesn't.

The word *jubilee* passed into the English language with only the meanings of joyfulness and celebration intact. The jubilant are full of jubilation. What stronger words can we conceive for giddy, full-bodied delight? The shepherds in "Angels We Have Heard on High" are asked, "Why this jubilee?" Why indeed! What do those poor nobodies who never mattered, except to a handful of bleating sheep, have to sing about? To those impoverished men whose homes were rocky, grassy fields out in the cold, who were exposed to the elements, Christ came before he came to anybody else.

Paul writes, "God loves a cheerful giver" (2 Cor. 9:7). The Greek word translated "cheerful" is *hilaros*, as in *hilarious*. We laugh, we revel in the joy of giving. It is a jubilee, and we are jubilant when our lives and resources are used in sync with God's very purpose in coming to earth. Jesus says, "Blessed are the meek, for they will inherit the earth" (Matt. 5:5). Blessed are the jubilant shepherds.

DAY 5

We Three Kings of Orient Are

*W*e three kings of Orient are; bearing gifts we traverse afar." At the very thought of them, I barely stifle a chuckle. My mind rushes to the hilarious scene in the Monty Python film *Life of Brian* where the magi mistakenly show up at the wrong house.

And we've all sat through our share of Christmas pageants. Three dads pressed into duty wearing bathrobes and cardboard crowns—probably giveaways at Burger King—squinting a little, gazing slightly upward, nodding, trying to look wise and regal while processing to the manger. I witnessed one pageant where the narrator reached the moment in the story when "they fell down and worshiped him" (Matt. 2:11, RSV), and one of the magi slipped and fell flat on his face, his fake gold coins clattering across the floor.

Matthew tells us the magi came "from the East" (2:1), perhaps Persia or Arabia or the Syrian desert. The Bible does not tell us they were wise. Following a star seems rather foolish, but I can only hope to be yet one more fool traipsing off after the Light of the world. They certainly were not kings, though mighty kings chronicled through history would one day bow down to the King of kings they sought. There you have it: theologically kooky humor at the very beginning of Jesus' story! A Libra, a Pisces, and a Taurus, gazing at their star charts, found Jesus, while Herod's scholars missed the Messiah entirely! How sobering. How many times have I flipped through the Bible, holding truth in my hands, yet still missing the living Lord? I know quite a few Bible facts—but am I personally acquainted with the real Jesus?

What did the magi see? A supernova? Jupiter and Saturn were in conjunction about that time. Some say Halley's comet passed not long before. Medieval writers believed the magi saw a bright angel, which they mistook for a star. "The First Noel" seems to think the star was so bright it was visible even by day: "It gave great light, and so it continued both day and night."

Bearing Gifts We Traverse Afar

During December I slip most easily into the role the magi played. I bear gifts. I traverse afar. The magi popped in with their gifts, then departed. They didn't stay close to the Lord Jesus like Joseph and Mary did. I wonder if I also keep some distance. I mean, I give Jesus a few gifts, pay my offering, say some prayers, read about the magi, take canned goods to the food collection—and then I go on my way.

I often fume about the commercialism of Christmas, and I could even blame the magi for kickstarting the whole notion of gift-giving at Christmas. Jesus did not remember their visit and therefore command, "Because I was born, you shall shop for one another on my birthday." Yet I find joy in seizing upon this season of the Lord's coming, traversing afar, and acting generously with those I love. Maybe the magi can teach us something about giving. What would a child do with gold or incense, much less myrrh? Theologians have suggested the gifts symbolize Jesus' royalty (gold), his divinity (frankincense), and his suffering (myrrh), but it's hard to say this was the magi's intent.

The magi brought gifts of immense value; they brought what was precious to them. They parted with what they adored to adore the Lord. We are not so wise in our giving. I traverse not far at all when I shop, since I shop online. Why? It's easier and more convenient for me. Or convenient for the recipient— hence the bane of gift cards, which say a lot about the giver (who hasn't bothered to think through the other person's life and snoop around to find something meaningful), and even more about our culture. We give cards. Why? "They should be able to get what they want." Notice that convenience was not a priority for the magi. Why has it become our guiding light?

I think of the times I have gone to considerable trouble to get just the right item, or times someone made something for me with her own hands. Not easy, not returnable, but profound. A few years back I got the idea of only giving things I already owned and not old stuff I didn't want any longer either. My precious possessions, offered to my loved ones.

The best gift I ever received was a pocketknife from an eighty-nine-year-old friend. He had carried it around in his pocket for decades, and he wanted me to have it. I had never asked for or even wanted a pocketknife. But it is precious to me because it was precious to him. And he added some words: "Carry this around in your pocket. One day, you'll be having a bad day, and when you do, feel that knife in your pocket and remember that somebody loves you."

This is the way God gives. God isn't Santa Claus, feverishly checking our request lists and sending the angels out to give what we ask for. God gives us much that is far better than our deepest desiring. God gives God's own self. Nobody asked for a baby born in a cow stall. But that is what God wanted to give. God knew that alone would express the depths of love we need.

You wouldn't need to be warned in a dream not to revisit nasty king Herod! But God lovingly warns the magi through a dream not to return to King Herod, and so they departed Jerusalem and "left for their own country by another road" (Matt. 2:12). They took a different highway—but I imagine Matthew winking a little, hoping we'll notice his subtle clue about what life is like once we've met Jesus. Nothing is the same. We may find ourselves going another way. T. S. Eliot ends his poem "The Journey of the Magi" imagining their thoughts as they returned home, "no longer at ease here, in the old dispensation, / With an alien people clutching their gods." Jesus does not make our lives more comfortable; Jesus doesn't help us fit in and succeed. We are no longer at ease in a world not committed to Jesus. A strange, unfamiliar road is now our path. But the road is going somewhere.

Hark! the Herald Angels

$\mathcal{A}$s we finish up our exploration of the male figures of the Advent season, let us turn to the angels. Even though the vast majority of angels topping our Christmas trees and crafted into figurines, jewelry, and statues are female, the biblical angels are overwhelmingly male. If there is such a thing as gender when it comes to heavenly beings, there must be quite a few female angels whose stories, like those of many earthly women, didn't make it into the Bible. At least we hope so, since we think of the angels singing, and God surely delights in rich four-part harmony.

During Advent we do hark to those "herald angels" singing, "Glory to the newborn King!" We sing of angels, but can we get quiet and hear them? "The world in solemn stillness lay, to hear the angels sing," "sweetly singing o'er the plains" that "glorious song of old." When Christmas arrives, we plead with them to sing even more for us: "Sing, choirs of angels, sing in exultation!" According to the Gospel of Luke, when the angels appear to the shepherds, one speaks. The angel says to them, "Do not be afraid" (Luke 2:10). "And suddenly there was with the angel a multitude of the heavenly host, praising God and saying, 'Glory to God'" (Luke 2:13-14). But surely the angels' praising involved singing as the carols suggest.

We don't for a moment think of an angel soloist. Angels sing together. And so for us, the most lovely witness of singing in worship is that all of us, young and old, sopranos, tenors, altos and basses, and those who aren't quite any of those, do it together. Finding unity at church may not be simple. But when we stand and sing all four stanzas of some hymn, we are mystically one.

Artists have imagined angels playing harps, "bending near the earth, to touch their harps of gold." Martin Luther King Jr. once composed a sermon on "How a Christian Overcomes Evil," using an illustration from mythology. Sirens sang seductive songs that lured sailors into shipwreck. Two men, however, managed to navigate those treacherous waters successfully, and King contrasted their techniques. Ulysses stuffed wax into the ears of his rowers, strapped himself to the mast of the ship, and by dint of will managed to steer clear of the shoals. But Orpheus, as his ship drew near the danger point, simply pulled out his lyre and played a song more beautiful than that of the Sirens, so his sailors listened to him instead of to them.[5] The beauty of our music during this season isn't sheer enjoyment. Good and evil are at stake.

Gabriel, the angel who spoke to Mary, was known in Judaism as a warrior against wickedness. He came to Mary not as a warrior but as a messenger. The word *angel* is derived from the Hebrew *mal'akh*, which means just that—"messenger." And we may chuckle or shrink back a little over Elie Wiesel's clever remark: "Whenever an angel says, 'Be not afraid!' you'd better start worrying. A big assignment is on the way."[6] In the Bible, angels show up with big assignments from God. Or questions about our lives. Origen, a theologian in the third century, believed we are assigned an angel at baptism, not to shelter us from harm but to hound us, to induce us to repent and be holy. Angels are all about communicating God's will, the breaking in of God's reign into our world, into our lives.

And remember the Bible's assignment to engage in radical hospitality: "Do not neglect to show hospitality to strangers, for by doing that some have entertained angels without knowing it" (Heb. 13:2). So the angels we encounter this Advent will be the homeless, the poor, the marginalized, the hurting, maybe even the untouchable. Can we show hospitality? Can we make room for the angels?

Their Watch of Wondering Love

If we think of angels praising, delivering messages from God, and breaking through our comfort zones, then we are a far cry from the angels of our culture, whether it's Clarence earning his wings, Victoria's Secret models, or television shows like "Touched by an Angel." According to the Bible, an angel's touch could make a woman pregnant or make a man walk with a limp (like Jacob; see Genesis 32). Do we really believe that angels are the ones who help us find our lost car keys or keep us from making wrong decisions?

"O Little Town of Bethlehem" tells us, "While mortals sleep, the angels keep their watch of wondering love." The angels are up all night; their watchful care never ceases. For the angels seem to dwell in some borderland between earth and heaven. In Jacob's dream, they ascend and descend between earth and heaven. So it is no surprise that at the most important moments in God's story, they are there. Early in Jesus' story, the angels are busy, announcing the pregnancy to Mary, calming Joseph in a dream, singing for the shepherds, and warning Joseph to get his family out of Bethlehem. After Jesus' death, they guard his tomb's entrance and declare, "He is not here, but has risen" (Luke 24:5). Angels bookend Jesus' story—they are the first witnesses to the Incarnation and Resurrection.

And yet, as serious as Gabriel, the archangel Michael, and the fierce host of angels in the book of Revelation might be, they seem lighthearted as well. They aren't God, after all. G. K. Chesterton said, "Angels can fly because they can take themselves lightly." I'm betting they sing not only sacred music but also secular songs—just for fun. Can we hear them harmonizing when we sing "Jingle Bells," "The Christmas Song," or even "I Saw Mommy Kissing Santa Claus"?

The Mother

William Wordsworth called Mary "our tainted nature's solitary boast." We might want to boast of a few other human beings, but Mary shows us what we need to know about mothering. She embodies the holiness and purpose to which we all might aspire, and she is the absolute closest flesh and blood has ever gotten to God. When we see Mary in art, sculpture, and drama, we see our fantasies imposed on her; and at the same time we come face-to-face with the dream of our noblest selves. Hail Mary, you truly are full of grace. Blessed are you among women, and blessed is the fruit of your womb, the Lord, for whose coming we wait.

DAY 1

Ave Maria

$\mathcal{A}$ve Maria" means "Hail, Mary," drawn from the angel Gabriel's greeting to Mary. He said, "Hail, Mary, full of grace, the Lord is with you." The sentence is repeated in one of the prayers of the rosary said by Catholics, but these words are not confined to Catholic practice. Gabriel surprised Mary, not just by showing up but also by speaking to her with immense respect, verging on deference.

Angels invade our human comfort zone and issue ridiculously big assignments. No assignment was bigger than Mary's—or more unlikely. And yet God comes to people who aren't seeking God at that moment. God calls a stunned person by name and then issues some huge, undoable order. The recipient of God's call, quite correctly, explains that the task is impossible. God asks Moses to outtalk the Pharaoh, but Moses is a stammerer. Jeremiah is summoned to overturn nations, but he's just a lad. Jonah is sent to convert the Ninevites, but he disavows the possibility, as the Ninevites are entirely too wicked for even God to reach. Isaiah is not holy enough. And now Mary is asked to bear a son in her womb. And yet she knows why this could not possibly be true. She has not been with any man, not even Joseph, her betrothed. God never seems to pick somebody with a multipage resume of spiritual accomplishment. If God says, "Do magnificent things for me!" we never hear a cocky reply, such as, "Of course I can do magnificent things for you." God chooses the unlikely. God assigns undoable tasks. God seems utterly uninterested in ability. What God wants is availability. During Advent, ask yourself, *Am I available for the coming of the Lord and whatever might be asked of me?*

Breath of Heaven

Until the angel shows up, Mary's future has been comfortably settled. Betrothed to Joseph, she risks everything by saying yes to the angel who invites her to bear not just *a* child but *this* child. Do neighbors avoid making eye contact with her? Joseph mercifully stays—but the birth to come? She might lose her life; she has seen other women die in childbirth. And her burden—to carry God's own son? Amy Grant's lovely "Breath of Heaven" echoes what must have been Mary's mood, as she is frightened by the burden she must bear. She pleads with this "breath of heaven" for guidance.

The angel comforts Mary: "Do not be afraid" (Luke 1:30). What is asked of Mary is unique, unprecedented, unfathomable; she serves as the intersection between earth and heaven, letting God take on flesh inside her, caring for this most precious of all children. And yet, isn't the same asked of us? Don't we live at the intersection of earth and heaven? Aren't we asked to let God take up residence in us? I wonder if an angel whispered to me last night and I missed it. Can we get quiet enough to hear? And maybe answer?

Mary hears the angel's words and immediately leaves on a journey to visit her cousin Elizabeth in faraway Ein Kerem. After that, she makes the journey to Bethlehem and later embarks on her arduous trek as a refugee to Egypt. In her lifetime, Mary would have traveled back and forth to Jerusalem many times, and if tradition is correct, she lived out her final years far north in Ephesus. When her son grows up, he calls fishermen away from their boats. "He said to them, 'Follow me. . . .' Immediately they left their nets and followed him" (Matt. 4:19-20). They have no idea where, not knowing what will unfold or how it will turn out. This is how we follow the one who comes in Advent: we go—we aren't sure where—knowing all is good as long as we stick close to him.

Today we speak casually about the presence of God. We assume that it is nice, soothing, encouraging, and affirming, a warm blanket wrapped around the life we've arranged for ourselves. Understandably we wish for such a presence from God. But this is like describing the ocean as calm, the wind as a whisper, or fire as warming. There can be—no, there *is* a terror to the presence of God. The fact that we sometimes feel this terror—its demand, its cost—is precisely the measure of how clearly we understand God.

Help Me Be Strong

The angel announces the new plan—Mary's old life is over. Perhaps she could have said no. We know she says yes: "Here am I, the servant of the Lord; let it be with me according to your word" (Luke 1:38). How beautiful, how courageous, how single-minded is her devotion. And her humility. In "Breath of Heaven," Mary asks if someone wiser or stronger should have taken her place—and then prays again for help and strength, offering all that she has and is.

Mary lets it be. She doesn't let her wishes stymie God's purpose. God's great adventure is like this for all of us. Most of our life with God is mundane—working, grocery shopping, watching TV, sitting in traffic. Can we know what it's all about, what it will all mean? When we look at children (and Christmas feels like a season for children), can we know what the scope of a single life might be or what God has envisioned? We can trust in God, we can believe in God, and that's our way of knowing. We "let it be," and then wait and see, perhaps never understanding. Yet ultimately we find the richness of the life God has given us in the mundane. Our tiny part in God's long-term plot of bringing all creation to its fulfillment seems insignificant, but it is only as insignificant as Mary putting oil in a lamp late one night so she can wipe the brow of her seven-year-old with a stomachache or trading a couple of coins for grain to bake a loaf of bread or staring out the window, wondering where her son had gone.

DAY 2

Isaiah 'Twas Foretold It

Through the centuries, artists have tried to paint or sculpt that shimmering moment when the angel comes to Mary and tells her that she will conceive a son and name him Jesus. Almost always, as the artists have reckoned it, she is holding an open book: God's Word, the Bible. The angel doesn't flit into her life in a vacuum. Mary is a student of God's Word, and when asked to become the mother of God, she replies, "Let it be with me according to your word" (Luke 1:38).

We are pretty sure Mary was illiterate. Certainly as a poor young woman, she didn't own a book; her family didn't have their own scripture scrolls. But she had seen the scrolls unfurled in the synagogue; she had listened attentively to the regular readings. Like most devout Jews, she had committed the Psalms and much more of scripture to memory.

Martin Luther called the Bible "the swaddling clothes in which Jesus is laid." To get near Mary and her son Jesus, to think their thoughts and love what they loved, we immerse ourselves in the scripture's stories, songs, laws, and prayers. For me to "let it be with me according to your word," I need to know God's Word. I need God's Word not to be like a novel I once read and stuck on a shelf when I was done. I need to know more than a verse or two. I need to study. But how do I begin? Maybe I begin with Mary and Jesus—with the Christmas story. I could procrastinate and hear it on Christmas Eve. But maybe I read right now. Can I work that in? Saint Augustine was converted when he heard a voice tell him, "Take up and read." For Jesus, I'll take it up and read.

Of Jesse's Lineage Coming

Jesus' birth story in Matthew's Gospel begins—with a genealogy? We might prefer a dramatic tease, something to lure us into the story instead of feeling like we're digging through someone else's family tree. Abraham begat Isaac, Isaac begat Jacob, and so on—forty-two begats in all "of Jesse's lineage coming." Each name in Matthew's genealogy represents a life—the miracle of birth, love, loss, labor, and death. Matthew acts like a librarian, walking us through the stacks, directing us to older books as he tells his story. The complex, baffling, and delightful stories of the people named in Jesus' genealogy are all drawn together into a grand story of God's life with us—and therefore even our stories find new homes with them.

Where did Jesus come from? Where did I come from? Inside me is the legacy of generations, the stamp of my DNA, the shape of my face and knobby knees. The family tree on which I find myself is lovely but gnarled, populated with saints and horse thieves, the pretty and the prickly. Am I free and in control? Or are the most decisive parts of me (skin color, nationality, gender, proclivity to disease, mental peculiarities) beyond my control? Am I here by accident or was it destiny? Who am I? What do I do next?

Most of Matthew's characters are men. He mentions only four women: Tamar, Rahab, Ruth, and Bathsheba. All four were strong women, but all four had questionable reputations in their day for various reasons. A fifth woman in the Gospel, Mary, mother of Jesus, was pregnant out of wedlock. Shouldn't God have designed a lineage for Jesus with virtuous women like Hannah and Miriam?

Jesus did not materialize out of nowhere. He was "long-expected . . . . Israel's strength and consolation," although the begetters in the genealogy didn't know precisely what they were longing for. Jesus' family tree was a mixed bag of heroes and commoners. We are begotten, birthed by God's love; we are mortal, noble, flawed, hopeful, longing for purpose. From such people Jesus came, and to such people he continues to come.

His Name Is Called Emmanuel

The elegant carol "Lo, How a Rose E'er Blooming" voices a fascinating Advent theme. "Isaiah 'twas foretold it"—but who was Isaiah? Was he a crystal ball, Nostradamus-type predictor of future events? Jerusalem was in political turmoil more than seven hundred years before Jesus was born. Ahaz was a clever king, though his faith was shallow, a prop for his political maneuvers.

Wars raged, factions swirled—and God sent Isaiah to invite Ahaz to trust God instead of his army and his allies abroad.

In a mystifying turn, Isaiah tells Ahaz of a "young woman" (the Hebrew original doesn't specify if she were a virgin or not) who would bear a son to be named "Immanuel." With the Assyrian army bearing down on the city, it doesn't do Ahaz much good to learn that in several hundred years a child would be born. Isaiah certainly means a particular woman Ahaz probably knows, someone in or near his palace. After all, the birth of any child is good cause to look to God instead of mere human force.

"The young woman . . . shall name him Immanuel" (Isa. 7:14). A curious name, unprecedented in those days, more a sermon than a mere name, bearing the profound truth of God's determination to be with us. That determination of God to be with us, in a season of war such as Ahaz's, or in our own day, is most fully and wonderfully embodied in the birth of Jesus. Isaiah foretold that God would be with Ahaz, with Mary and Joseph, and with you and me, always.

Western society says everything is up to you: You've got to make it happen; you must be spiritual; you must be good, generous, hard-working, loving, diligent—since meaning derives from within you. Isaiah foretells a better day, a richer hope, when meaning comes from outside ourselves and it isn't up to each individual. It's all gift, all grace, God with us, God never leaving us to our own devices or alone.

DAY 3

Mother and Child

She gave birth to her firstborn son and wrapped him in bands of cloth, and laid him in a manger" (Luke 2:7). Divine beauty, the fullness of truth, the love we've known and craved and tried to give, our very destiny—it's all there in a mother's arms encircling her newborn son. Peek over a new mother's shoulder as she caresses her child.

Maybe you've been in that most beautiful curled-up circle yourself. But, of course, you have been! You once were that small, that vulnerable and needy. Someone held you, and you've never been closer to God than in that moment. A mother's cradling of new life is the clearest possible window into God's heart. God thought, *I want them to know me—so I will do this. I will be born and tenderly embraced by my mother, just like all of them.*

I wonder what Jesus' birth was like. I'm fond of envisioning it the way Rembrandt did in his "Adoration of the Shepherds," with glowing chiaroscuro. The reality must have been far scarier. Onlookers did what they could, but they must have shuddered over the loss of blood, with no antibiotics or pain relievers, no suctioning of the infant's lungs, no physician nearby. When Jesus was born, Mary and Joseph must have been relieved she had survived. They must have held their breath during those agonizing seconds before Jesus' first cry—which Madeleine L'Engle suggested might have sounded "like a bell."[7] Perhaps Mary held him to her breast, voiced a prayer of gratitude. Mary nursed him, toyed with his fingers, sang to him, and rocked him, beamed with pride when onlookers gazed into their tightly knit realm of tender love.

Round Yon Virgin

Rembrandt was right to capture the stillness, light and shadow, love and adoration, holiness and revelation surrounding the infant Jesus' first moments. On Christmas Eve, we begin lighting candles as we sing these familiar, moving strains of "Silent Night": "Holy night, all is calm, all is bright." Normally our nights are busy, frittered away, or spent in exhaustion—hardly holy. Where is the night holy, calm, and bright? "Round yon virgin, mother and child," that's where. When else in the year do we say *round* meaning "around"? And when else would we say an old-fashioned word like *yon*? And yet on the night of all nights, we sing with tender affection and joy both "round" and "yon."

Mother—and child. Could there be a more intimate bond between two human beings, the child having taken up residence not near but actually inside the mother, growing, receiving nourishment, loved before even being seen, causing considerable discomfort and yet eliciting great hope? Who cut the umbilical cord between Jesus and Mary? Joseph? The umbilical cord may be cut, but the deep bond of mother and child cannot be severed. Or can it?

I found myself reduced to unexpected tears when I saw the film version of Anna Quindlen's novel *One True Thing*. Ellen (played by Renée Zellweger) leaves her life and career to come home to care for her mother (played by Meryl Streep) who is dying of cancer. Knowing this will be their last Christmas together, they venture out into the cold for the community Christmas tree lighting. The choir leads the singing of "Silent Night," and Ellen's mother joins in with what strength she can muster, defiantly declaring, "All is calm, all is bright."

Then the women sing words we all know but with a poignancy that buckles the knees: "Mother and child." The carol means Mary and Jesus. But the tender love of Mary and Jesus is echoed in the affection of every mother and child in every age and place. Here they are, two grown women, singing of the mother and child of the first Christmas now in their last Christmas as mother and child.

Such scenes make us sad and happy all at once. Some unutterable joy lies hidden in the sorrowful tears. Life is a paradox—shadow and light—like the Rembrandt painting. Especially at Christmas, we may know an intensity of joy and hope but also a peculiar kind of sorrow, a sense of loss for who isn't there, loves lost or that never were.

I wonder if we can conceive of all who have ever been mother and child as round yon virgin and near the Christ child. Can we know healing, gratitude, a lost past recovered, love redeemed? Those candles raised in a Christmas Eve service form, for me, the most beautiful moment of the year. The symbolism is perfect, for even the flicker of a modest candle banishes the darkness. And no darkness can overcome the delicate yet unbreakable love of mother and child—Mary and Jesus, and you and your own mother.

When the light of the world dawned inside Mary's body and was then enveloped in her arms, we finally see our true selves and the true soul of God in the glow. I admire this Ethiopian prayer to Mary from the ninth century: "Your hands touched him who is untouchable and the divine fire within him. Your fingers are like the incandescent tongs with which the prophet received the coal of the heavenly offering. You are the basket bearing this burning bread and you are the cup of this wine. O Mary, . . . we most earnestly pray to you . . . that, just as . . . water is not divided from . . . wine, so we may not separate ourselves from your son, the lamb of salvation."[8]

Holy Infant So Tender and Mild

"Silent night, holy night." "Infant holy, infant lowly." "Holy infant so tender and mild." During December, we sing the word *holy* often enough to lead us to believe there is something *holy* about Christmas. I suspect that thinking of Mary and Jesus as the essence of holiness will tap deeply into our innate desire to be holy. Mary wasn't perfect, but she kept her mind focused on God. She avoided things not pleasing to God, and she strove for a match between the will of God and her actions. Daily routine is more than actions, as is holiness. She examined her motives, she thought carefully about God before she acted, and she imagined her body to be a vessel for God to dwell in and to use.

Jesus' first Christmas gift was the holy, tender face of his mother. Maybe this is holiness: being seen by Jesus, being aware of his loving presence. Then I wish to be nothing but holy. I want my thinking, words, and actions to reflect the gaze of his face. "The Lord make his face to shine upon you" (Num. 6:25). Perhaps this will be our prayer this Advent season.

DAY 4

How a Rose E'er Blooming

"I am a rose of Sharon, a lily of the valleys" (Song of Sol. 2:1). So says the ardent lover in the Bible's elegant love poem, a riveting dialogue between two would-be lovers. Desire is celebrated; passion is championed. The body is not only a temple for the Holy Spirit but also a bungalow for human pleasure. Or perhaps one of the ways the Spirit dwells in the body is through physical pleasure.

We do not know how the Holy Spirit came upon Mary's body and planted new life in her womb. Did she suffer morning sickness? Were feelings of delight stirring inside her as she carried the fetus growing inexorably into an infant?

Language often fails us when we try to describe tender beauty—and what could be more beautiful than young Mary making herself fully available to God, risking her secure future with Joseph, feeling sickness and fatigue as the new life inside her grows, suffering the pangs of labor, hearing the baby's first cry, then cradling him, nursing him, counting his fingers?

Hymns like "Lo, How a Rose E'er Blooming" give voice to such beauty.

Mary's delicate love and the child's fragile splendor are both compared to a rose, the most praised of all flowering things, perfectly symbolic of beauty and vulnerability—and yet peril and pain. Roses, hard to grow, the petals such thin wonders, strike awe as we hover near each blossom—yet they possess thorns that pierce. Is Mary the rose in the carol? Or is it Jesus? Or both of them, the way a mother and her infant are really one, not two?

And who was pierced? Jesus, yes—but that is to leap ahead thirty years when he was pierced, as was his mother who watched the crucifixion helplessly, in unspeakable agony. She had been warned—or perhaps we should say prepared: When Mary and Joseph took the baby Jesus to the temple for purification and circumcision, an old devout man, Simeon, spoke ominously to Mary: "A sword will pierce your own soul" (Luke 2:35). Every mother anticipates some heartbreak. But whose heartbreak was more shattering than Mary's?

Christina Rossetti picked up on the image of the rose in her lovely poem about Mary:

> Herself a rose, who bore the Rose,
> She bore the Rose and felt its thorn.
> All Loveliness new-born
> Took on her bosom its repose,
> And slept and woke there night and morn.

To Show God's Love Aright

Why did Mary so humbly bear this child who would never really be hers but God's? As the hymn intones, "to show God's love aright, she bore to us a Savior." To show God's love *aright*. How often is God's love shown *a-wrong*? We might fantasize of a God who is indulgent, not minding at all how we live, but such laid back love on earth is a lazy masquerade of attentive love. Sometimes we are told God's love is rather stingy—very real but limited, bestowed only on certain folks. Such a God is no God but nothing more than humanity at its narrowest. Many believe God's love to be something that can be earned; aren't we weary of laboring away in a culture that is all about earning? Our true hearts desire mercy, grace—precisely what Mary gave Jesus, the very miracle God comes with, no, that God comes *as* at Christmas.

Often we wish God's love were a blanket of sweet protection against all difficulties, a hovering love that erases sorrow and shields us from peril. But like the helicopter parent, such a controlling God would rob us of our personhood and steal away with our chances to learn and to give care to those who are hurting. In a materialist culture, especially at Christmas, we confuse God's love with things. Mary and Joseph had nothing much but their love, care, and barely enough food and shelter to give the Master of the universe. That reality gives us a hint that "enough" isn't as much as we think; it is an invitation to live more simply and to share so that other holy families might have enough.

Plenty of us think a-wrongly that God's love is remote or impossible to access. But the whole wonder of Advent is that

God could not contain God's self in heaven but came to earth as a baby, as intimate as a child at his mother's breast, as close as the breath you just took, the beating of your heart in your chest even now.

Learning to Love

If you ever worry you will miss God's love or misunderstand what it's like, go back to the manger, to Mary, and Jesus, the rose, God's love shown aright. Then something changes—or maybe everything. In my favorite animated movie, *Beauty and the Beast*, a rich young man receives an enchanted rose from an old beggar woman. He sneers at the gift and turns her away. She warns him not to judge by appearances. She isn't an old beggar woman at all but an enchantress who turns him into a beast, informing him that the enchanted rose will bloom until his twenty-first birthday. If he can learn to love before the last petal falls from the rose on that day, the spell will be broken.

Disney movies have predictably happy endings. For us during Advent, the question is when will we learn to love? Yes, television, novels, and people we chat with at work would all agree that everyone just knows how to love already, innately. The learning curve, once we've encountered the rose e'er blooming, mother and child, seems steep, but God makes it easy if we know where to look. And God's love is so appealing we will never want to go back to love a-wrong.

I like to imagine what Paul thought of Mary's love for Jesus and of Jesus' love for her when he wrote, "I will show you a still more excellent way. . . . Love is patient; love is kind; love is not envious or boastful or arrogant or rude. It does not insist on its own way; it is not irritable or resentful; it does not rejoice in wrongdoing, but rejoices in the truth. It bears all things, believes all things, hopes all things, endures all things. Love never ends" (1 Cor. 12:31–13:8). And Mary certainly did bear all things. She saw her son speak like a child and then become a man. Late in her life, when Jesus had been gone for so many years, did she long for the day she would see him again face-to-face?

DAY 5

The Virgin Mother Kind

"Round yon virgin," "the Virgin Mother kind," "offspring of a virgin's womb," "Lo, he shuns not the Virgin's womb." During Advent we sing joyfully of the Virgin. "Before [Mary and Joseph] lived together, she was found to be with child from the Holy Spirit" (Matt. 1:18). We modern people wonder. Critics of Christianity scoff. Is this idea of her virginity mere metaphor? Did the biblical writers latch onto the idea to enhance Jesus' divinity?

Never have I been asked, "Pastor, do you really believe in Jesus?" or "Do you really believe in the forgiveness of sins?" Yet quite a few times I have been asked, "Do you really believe in the virgin birth?" I wonder why. The question probably says far more about us than about Mary.

My answer when asked is, "I really do believe Mary was a virgin and that Jesus was conceived by the Holy Spirit. I can't explain the biology of it; I'm not sure I even think of it in a gynecological way, but I do believe it." Believing this doesn't get me into heaven and doesn't keep you out if you don't. But I believe it.

My reasons are curious even to me. I have tried to think about the twenty or thirty people who have lived on this earth that I admire the most—saints, heroes, people whose behavior I wish to mimic, people whose wisdom and prayerfulness I want a small taste. If we could interview any one of them and ask, "Do you believe Mary was a virgin?" each one would say, "Of course, yes."

This proves nothing, but I find myself in community with these saints. I want a piece of the relationship they enjoy with God. So if the virginity of Mary mattered to Saint Francis, Mother Teresa, my grandfather, and others of their ilk, then believing this can't be the ruin of me. So I choose to stand not with the skeptics but with the company of saints who have blessed us all.

Speaking of skepticism: If we sneer at the idea of a virgin birth, it may be because we modern people have trouble believing anything much beyond what we can control, measure, or do for ourselves. We have science, and we understand physical cause and effect. But is everything reducible to cause and effect?

I hope in, I believe in, and I have even experienced a deeper, inexplicable dimension to life. I believe God loves me and you and God's world enough to get involved, that God lifts a gentle, powerful finger and dips down into our limited perspective and does some good we didn't do for ourselves. God does things we couldn't dream of achieving. I prefer not to be the kind of person who says Mary couldn't have been a virgin because we are so smart and we grasp cause and effect regarding how all babies find their way into the world. Maybe Jesus' birth is the exception that proves the rule. Or perhaps it is the author of this child Jesus' birth that secretly sets in motion the cause and effect that wrought you and me, who are thus not stuck with mere fate or what we can do on our own.

He Shuns Not the Virgin's Womb

And then there is this: For the earliest Christians, the virgin birth was a way of underlining Jesus' humanity, not his divinity! The shock for ancient people was that anything divine could be born at all so having a virgin as mother would have been a minimal expectation. The shock for us is if anybody is a virgin.

People have tried to tell me that the virginity of Mary doesn't matter in modern times, and I find myself responding that the virginity of Mary matters more in modern times than at any other point in history. I hope valiantly something like virginity matters and is even possible. When Mary bore Jesus, she was probably fourteen or fifteen in a culture that attached great shame to premarital sex. We on the other hand don't attach shame to much of anything. Coddled by a tawdry media, teenagers and frankly all-aged grownups engage in sex as something recreational, not as a careful stewarding of God's holy gift to us.

God is not an anti-sex deity. The good God who loves us more than we love ourselves and fashioned our bodies for pleasure and holiness has wired us for the highest delights and the deepest joy. God created sex as perhaps the most scintillating gift to us, most richly understood when we embrace sex in a lifelong, committed relationship. I have counseled so many people whose most gut-wrenching wounds in life have arisen because they frittered away that most precious, intimate part of themselves, squandering their glory with someone who didn't stick around.

The year before last I married a couple who had never had sex with anyone. They were virgins, and they entered their marriage with a profound delight, a sense of pride and integrity, honoring each other (and God!). The church still has something to say about sexual ethics, not so we might condemn, but because we love people and want only the finest for them. Virginity is not a lack, the missing out on something. Virginity is good. Jesus "shuns not the Virgin's womb."

A reporter once pushed his microphone toward Mother Teresa and asked, "Mother, why are you so holy?" She responded, "You talk as if holiness were abnormal. Holiness is normal. To be anything else is to be abnormal. Why aren't you asking unholy people why they are unholy?"[9] Of course, we are all unholy. But we have good cause to look for and dare to live into instances of holiness. It is the dark underside of us that scoffs at the notion of Mary's virginity or could simply care less. It is the noble image of God in us that hopes she was and believes and then even takes fumbling but determined steps to let holiness happen in our lives as well.

DAY 6

Thou Long-Expected Jesus

For Mary, at the very outset of her adventure with God, waiting is involved. She would have known those great phrases from the Psalms, like "I wait for the LORD, my soul waits" (Ps. 130:5), and from the Prophets too: "Those who wait for the LORD shall renew their strength" (Isa. 40:31). Israel waited centuries for Jesus; Mary waited nine months. Mary wouldn't have detected the nuances in the English word "wait," but we can. We "wait" upon the Lord, and we "wait" on the Lord.

First: we wait. It takes time. When? Today? Not today. You have to wait nine months, thankfully, for a baby to arrive. We are no good at waiting. Children can hardly wait for Christmas morning. We tense up at a long traffic light. The long weekend before the doctor can say "malignant" or "benign" is ploddingly slow. God seems slow—but we wait. "My soul waits for the Lord more than those who watch for the morning" (Ps. 130:6).

But "waiting" is also what a "waiter" does in a restaurant. "Those who wait on the Lord" are those who get busy and find out what the Lord needs or is asking. Waiting isn't passive. Active waiting, during Advent, means to be preparing for what is to come, even if we do not know what all is to come. Once Jesus came, Mary certainly waited on him, the one she had been waiting for.

Mary waited the rest of her life, patiently, carrying on with the mundane tasks before her, feeding, caring for a growing son, nursing his scrapes and fevers, cleaning, cooking, sewing, weary most days, enduring the death of her husband, keeping the lamps burning in the dark, gathering supplies, fixing little leaks in the thatched roof. She waited during the long years Jesus was away, teaching, healing, risking life and limb, wondering when and if he might come home, realizing in her midforties that he was gone for good. She waited during those harrowing hours he hung on the cross. Whose wait for Easter morning was longer than Mary's? Into old age she waited: others were celebrating and a great body of believers were scattering around the globe in his name. She alone felt the sorrow of missing the one she'd held so close and known before and better than anybody else.

With Mary We Behold It

At some point, on a day we know nothing about, Mary breathed her last, and was buried. Catholics eventually were taught that she was "assumed" into heaven. What they also have believed is that Mary waited around for a while, and then showed up again, and again. In the fifth century, in Rome, even though it was the sweltering month of August, out of the blue it snowed—and Mary appeared to a rich husband and wife, the first of many manifestations of Mary over the centuries to various pious people all over the world. We may scoff, or chalk it up to excessive piety. But if God's people live eternally with God, and still care for us, and if we're talking about the very person who bore God in her own womb, why should she not be in a position to communicate with God's people down here? Our carols imagine Mary as here with us, now.

During Advent of 1531, an Aztec peasant named Juan Diego was on his way to church—the date being significant, since Christianity had only shown up in Aztec lands a mere forty years earlier! Mary appeared as an Aztec maiden and spoke Juan's dialect, saying, "I am your merciful mother. I listen to lamentations and remedy miseries."

Over the centuries, Mary has appeared at Fátima, Portugal, Syracuse, Sicily, Medgujorge, Yugoslavia, and a handful of other places. Some "appearances" we'd count as hokey and ridiculous, others compelling and relatively authenticated, if such things can be authenticated. In 1858, Mary appeared several times to a fourteen-year-old French girl named Bernadette Soubirous. Thousands of gallons of water flow from the spot where Bernadette interacted with Mary, and thousands claim to have been cured in the streams of the shrine there, in Lourdes.

A few years ago, a friend of mine spent a week in Lourdes. When she returned, I asked her, "Did you see any miracles?" She said, "Oh yes, every day." "Every day? Tell me!" She explained: "Every day at Lourdes, no matter who you are or where you are from or what's wrong with you, you are welcomed and loved."

Mary would like that, as would her son, Jesus. Refugees adore Mary, for she had to flee to Egypt to save her family. The oppressed love the song she sang about the rich and powerful being defeated (see Luke 1:46-55) and sing it with vigor. Mary lives on.

Our True Mother

What is the afterlife of anyone? Of your own mother? Or your grandmother? On Mother's Day, our thoughts veer toward the sentimental; we can get a bit sappy. But the real greatness of a mother is akin to that of Mary. In sustaining memory, in ongoing presence, in unfailing impact, a mother, a grandmother can bring joy and courage decades after being buried. Or think of the aggrieved mothers, the pained but powerful company of mothers who stand up and protest, the mothers of the murdered activists of the Plaza de Mayo in Buenos Aires, Argentina, the mothers of Palestinian and Israeli children who could settle the political dispute if we'd take their sorrows into account, all the Rachels of history, weeping over their children sacrificed on the pyres of crass power plays and evil chicanery.

For me, one of the most poignant and provocative thoughts about Mary and mothers and Jesus comes from the pen of the medieval mystic, Julian of Norwich. Her visions of Jesus pulsate with powerful love and tender comfort—and no passage moves me as much as when Julian explains that "Jesus Christ . . . is our true Mother. We have our being from him . . . Our true Mother Jesus . . . bears us for joy . . . He carries us within him in love and travail." His motherhood involves love, wisdom, and protection. Jesus our Mother "feeds us with his own self." When we are ashamed, Jesus our Mother "does not wish us to flee away." No, "he then wants us to behave like a child," who runs quickly to its mother and calls to its mother for help: "My kind Mother, my gracious Mother, my beloved Mother, have mercy on me. I . . . cannot make it right except with your help and grace."[10]

Jesus learned the wonder of mothering from Mary. And the pledge to all of us, especially during the Advent season when we feel the pangs of family dysfunction or grieve the loss of mothers and other loved ones, is that Jesus can be mother, sister, brother, and father to us who need family, grace, and belonging at the deepest core of our beings.

The Child

*F*inally we come to the child Advent has been seeking. Each prayer in Charles Wesley's "Come, Thou Long-Expected Jesus" is eloquent, and necessary for our spiritual wellbeing: "From our fears and sins release us, let us find our rest in thee. . . . Rule in all our hearts alone; . . . raise us to thy glorious throne."

These prayers can be and will be answered because of the paradox of the incarnation: "Born a child and yet a King." If the world had invented a savior, it would have devised a mighty warrior who would crush evildoers or a wealth manager to make everyone rich and powerful. But God became small for us in Christ; God showed us God's heart so our hearts might be won. It isn't that Christ was really a powerful commander who merely pretended to be a child, humble and vulnerable. Christ showed us that the true heart of God has no desire to trump enemies; God loves, embraces, and risks everything hoping we will love God and each other.

In Christ we see a different kind of power—the kind we notice when a baby is born and we find ourselves gently cooing and tenderly cradling a fragile life and hope of the future. A baby keeps us up at night, yet we find no inconvenience too great to bear. During Advent we pray for the long-expected Jesus' coming. He comes in no other form than as a child we must care for, who insists we shed our mightiness and offer love instead.

DAY 1

Mild He Lays His Glory By

*A*dvent is the season when we look for the coming of the Lord. This coming down of God to earth, this impossible, scandalous wonder, is given the theological term *incarnation*. "The Word became flesh and lived among us . . . full of grace and truth" (John 1:14). Words elude us when we try to describe this miracle of all miracles. Some of the finest language mustered to portray the incarnation can be found in the carols we sing in December.

We might consider "Mild he lays his glory by." When we see someone "lay his glory by," it's never done mildly. Athletes caught cheating, celebrities misbehaving, and politicians exposed as corrupt lay down whatever ephemeral glory they might have with a thud, a clang, with blushing, attorneys scrambling, tabloids drooling.

In Charles Wesley's "Hark! the Herald Angels Sing," Jesus laid his glory by—how? *Mild*. Modern English has hollowed out the word *mild*, so to us it feels like "bland" or "unexciting." But *mild* has traditionally been defined as "gracious, merciful, conciliatory." There is even an ancient English usage of *mild* as "softly radiant." God resided rather grandly in the unimaginably marvelous corridors of heaven—but laid his glory by graciously (to be grace for us), mercifully, and with the sole purpose of reconciliation.

Was Wesley right about "laying his glory by"? Paul had Christmas in mind when he spoke of Christ, "who, though he was in the form of God . . . emptied himself . . . being born in human likeness" (Phil. 2:6-7). Nowadays some scholars dare to translate this not "*Although* he was in the form of God" but "*Because* he was in the form of God he emptied himself." Indeed. When Jesus was born, he was fully God; he didn't take a temporary detour from his true self by being born in Bethlehem. Jesus showed us the heart of God most spectacularly—as a humble nobody, sleeping in the most ignoble quarters, consorting with questionable people, laying down his life, bearing shame, and abandoning all privilege. God's signature, the truest manifestation of the glory of God, came in that first cry, before the umbilical cord was cut, in the messiness of human existence.

Why Lies He in Such Mean Estate?

Another of our favorite carols "What Child Is This" is set to the tune "Greensleeves." One of its several profound phrases is a question: "Why lies he in such mean estate?" Only in recent decades has *mean* come to denote "cruel" or "malicious." Originally *mean* meant the middle, moderation, the absence of extremes. For Chaucer, *mean* was used for a go-between, a mediator. In the late Middle Ages, Jesus was spoken of as the "mean," the mediator between us and God.

How did Jesus become this "mean," our beloved go-between? *Mean*, beginning as the "middle," began to signify "common," or "normal," but then—not surprisingly, given human inclinations to devise caste systems and to identify haves and have-nots—*mean* slipped into "inferior, undistinguished, of low, despised rank." Why lies he in such mean estate? Our go-between loves humility; God, in the hallowed depths of God's own heart, is humble, so Christ's "mean estate" simply tells the truth about God.

God also wanted to save everybody, not just the rich, agile, well-connected, or spiritually astute. The lowly, those the world may despise, are special treasures in God's mind. God chose to lie "in such mean estate" in order to be a mirror in which we discern our own humility, our lowliness, the simple truth about ourselves as dependent beings who are small, fragile, mortal. When we think we are in charge, invincible, doing quite well on our own, we miss the golden "mean," the go-between's rescue, the mediator's grace.

And one last thing—we sing "Why lies he in such mean estate?" not "Why does he stand and flex his muscles in such mean estate?" When Jesus came, he lay down. He was an infant who couldn't hold up his head or sit up. He could only lie in the manger or in Mary's caressing arms. Infants rest. Infants are vulnerable. They never overpower, except in the way they elicit tenderness, cooing, gentleness. Any time we lie down, we embody this spiritual wisdom: "Be still, and know that I am

God" (Ps. 46:10). To lie down, we must feel secure. Lying down is the posture of trust. Jesus was vulnerable because he seeks love, he doesn't overwhelm, he never manipulates or coerces or intimidates. That is why he lay down in the manger, why he laid down his life, why his defining moment was when he could no longer hold up his head but lay down in the tomb. Because he laid down and became the "mean," the mediator, now we can lie down every night in faith; we can even lie down at the end of life confident in the one who lay down his life for us.

DAY 2

The Christmas Song

Once he was grown up, Jesus was fascinated by children and seemed eager for us to be as well. He was single and had no children of his own. But he refused to let them be hushed or squirreled away so he could do his work. Children were his work. All of us barely hanging on to our childlike souls are his work. To us he said, "Unless you change and become like children, you will never enter the kingdom of heaven" (Matt. 18:3). Jesus was the Word made flesh. God came to us not as a giant or an intimidating warrior. God came as something each of us once was: a small, vulnerable child. The more we can go back, the more we can remember very early moments in our lives, the more we observe children closely and enter their world, the closer we come to what God showed us in Jesus.

Although it's not a religious carol, "The Christmas Song" revels in much of what we need to know about the coming of the Lord. I do not recall roasting chestnuts on any open fire, but even in the thick of the December rush, I am more likely to slow down and enjoy the December rush. I am more likely to make something, to cook something, to step back in time before technology engulfed everything, before we thought it was a clever idea to pay for things we are capable of doing ourselves. As adults we have lost our ability to wonder. When was the last time your jaw dropped over some simple marvel?

Children can teach us. My tiny tots (when they were still tiny) were held spellbound by simple pleasures. My wife and I would wrap up spectacular presents for our children—but what would capture their fancy? The wrapping paper. Hardly noticing the purchased gift, my children would walk around proudly with the bow I had stuck on the package and finger the colorful ribbon for hours. It doesn't matter what's in the box because it's the love, the hugs, the eyes flown open, the giddy anticipation that keeps you awake in the dark—and you don't mind if you sing off-key or what anything cost, or even if you're cold.

Gifts can be found all around—in our backyards, crackling in the fireplace, in the warmth of a scarf, in the face of a child or a grown-up—and we need not wait until Christmas morning to enjoy them.

Yea, Lord, We Greet Thee

What a thrill it is when we jubilantly sing, "O come, all ye faithful. . . . O come, let us adore him, Christ the Lord" on Christmas Eve. When we awaken the next morning, shouldn't our first thought be, "Yea, Lord, we greet thee, born this happy morning"? The Lord comes. How do we greet him? I love the Italian film *The Gospel According to St. Matthew* by Pasolini, which depicts the Magi arriving in Bethlehem by day. They smile, take the baby in their arms, lift him up, laugh. They greet him as you would any newborn child. Do we greet the Lord with dull solemnity or giddy delight?

How would we greet the Christ child? In the biblical world, the common greeting would be *Shalom!*—"Peace." To utter *Shalom* is not merely good manners. The word invokes divine power, a blessing, a dream of peace, a holy love, a prayer for the palpable presence of God. We greet our Lord, putting our best foot forward, hoping he will see us not as we see ourselves but in the light of eternity as those deeply loved.

Maybe he will see the true image of God in us. We greet the Lord with smiles. We say *Shalom*, with the resonances ringing— and we notice a hand held out. We take it, a greeting, a sign of affection, a firm bond . . . and we vow never ever to let go.

No Crying He Makes

If we lingered with this Christ child for a few hours, what would we see and hear? A legend emerged during the early years of Christianity that when Jesus was born, there was total, utter silence— everywhere—for an hour. No one spoke, dogs did not bark, crickets were silent. Charming and theologically profound—but unlikely. I imagine a fair amount of unpleasant racket in that manger. "The cattle are lowing" might have been the most melodious of the sounds. Sheep baaa-ing, the crowd pressing into Bethlehem being met with "No Vacancy" signs—and a baby's cry.

We love "Away in a Manger," and we may forgive its author for holding Jesus in such high regard that he imagined him not even crying. "But little Lord Jesus, no crying he makes." Surely he cried! God became like us: We cry, so Jesus cried. Babies cry, and for that we are grateful because that sound is the sign of life, vitality, a protest against being so rudely removed from the warm safety of the womb, a declaration to the world that "I have arrived!" And it wouldn't be Jesus' last cry; he wept over the city, over the death of his friend Lazarus, and he probably still weeps over us since he loves us so much.

Jesus' very name is a cry. The Hebrew *yeshua* means "Help!" Mothers in the intense agony of childbirth would cry out *yeshua*! Did Mary? Surely the pain was intense, this delivery of new life. Mary cried out; Jesus cried out; and in that scream in the dark, help dawned for us. Jesus, this *yeshua*, is the answer to the cry of humanity across the ages. He alone can help, and he does help.

"Away in a Manger" shares with us the best conceivable prayer in its third stanza, one we may pray during Advent and for the rest of our lives: "Be near me, Lord Jesus, I ask thee to stay close by me forever, and love me, I pray; bless all the dear children in thy tender care, and fit us for heaven to live with thee there." This is the coming of the Lord. This is our salvation. Jesus is near. And he came to take us home to heaven where we will live with him forever. For that we hope even now to be fit.

DAY 3

Dear Desire of Every Nation

$\mathcal{A}$ fascinating phrase Charles Wesley used to extol Jesus in "Come, Thou Long-Expected Jesus" has a global resonance: "Dear desire of every nation." Was Wesley naive? Countless nations couldn't care less about Jesus. In every nation, Jesus is ridiculed by many and trivialized even by the Christians who queue up outside malls and clamor to garner more stuff, exposing the sad truth that our desire is for things and not the Lord Jesus.

Yet I remember a thought from C. S. Lewis: "It would seem that Our Lord finds our desires not too strong, but too weak. We are half-hearted creatures, fooling about with drink and sex and ambition when infinite joy is offered us, like an ignorant child who wants to go on making mud pies in a slum because he cannot imagine what is meant by the offer of a holiday at the sea. We are far too easily pleased."[11] Perhaps nations are too easily pleased. Nations want power, security, and vigorous economies. None of this is inherently evil, but perhaps something deeper is missed. What about a nation being good or being the catalyst for the good of other nations? What about being a nation that lifts up the neediest, a nation that honors God—even if we value the coexistence of various religions? Though Christianity is just one of many faiths, perhaps its virtue is that it worships a child who grew up to preach goodness and peace, who did not annihilate foes but loved them. The question posed in Psalm 2:1—"Why do the nations conspire, and the peoples plot in vain?"—might be answered by this long-awaited Jesus, the secret and "dear desire of every nation."

The Lord came when the nations were powerful. Caesar Augustus was the greatest of Rome's emperors, Herod the greatest of Judea's kings. Tourists still visit their monuments. If we could travel back in time and interview them, they would chuckle over the idea of Jesus being their Lord. Could we convince them that the deep purpose of their kingdoms was not their own wealth and glory but his—his peace and glory? But we know the hidden plot of God working among all the nations, even among those who do not know or seek the Lord.

Some Children See Him

James Taylor favored all of us by recording "Some Children See Him," one of several lovely carols written by Alfred Burt, who died in 1954 without having achieved any commercial success. The carol's insight is simple: There are some children who see Jesus as fair, with soft hair, while others see him with darker skin and hair. Yet other children see him with almond eyes and olive skin. All love him! This is the gospel. Children in every place will see the baby Jesus' face as being like their own, glowing with grace, full of holy light.

How shrewd of God to ensure that the holy birth took place at the intersection of multiple continents—not in Africa or Asia or Europe but at the meeting point of them all. How wise of God not to be white or black but of a hue different from but kin to all of us. God comes to us where we are, as we are, not merely to bless us but to leave us forever changed. God comes to transform us, to take us somewhere.

The gospel comes to us in this way or not at all. We hear first in our own tongue; God shows us our own face in God's holy face. God does this to stop us in our tracks, so we might figure out that many of our most treasured convictions are just plain wrong, and we've missed out on all the joy. This U-turn of the mind then becomes our conversion, which isn't a matter of good intentions but a miracle wrought by God—the God who is infinitely flexible to meet each one of us where we are. God's love is just as infinite and miraculous in its effects. And so we have compelling cause to think of the nations from the viewpoint of God, who wove the divine image and even the desire for the coming of the Lord into every soul in every place.

And the Soul Felt Its Worth

If we had a checklist for this season, it probably would include sitting on a crowded pew listening to a soloist's rendition of "O Holy Night." How odd: a song we love that we may never have sung together. We listen. Among its many fine phrases, we hear this: "'Til He appeared, and the soul felt its worth." Society measures worth by salary, real estate, portfolio, and countless other status markers. Jesus, born to very poor parents, himself homeless for some time, "despised and rejected" (Isa. 53:3), does not seem to notice and certainly is not impressed.

How fantastic are you? Look at your fingers, your skin, hair. Feel your pulse, notice your breathing. Feel the weariness in your feet or the hunger in your stomach.

God said, "I will be like that. Human life is the perfect vehicle for me to be me, to exhibit my heart, to reveal my mind." As a human being I have immeasurable worth because God joined God's own self to who I am, who you are, to the stranger, the one you love, the one who broke your heart, even the one who doesn't believe. We think of Jesus' wise teaching or his healing touch or certainly his crucifixion and resurrection as extraordinary, as saving us. But his very appearing, his showing up on earth—this is God's stupendous adventure to love us, to save us, to bring us home.

"'Til He appeared, and the soul felt its worth": the order is everything. We do not submit a resume of worth to God, and then God appears. No, God appears, and while we might blush a little over the two-bit life we were leading before we noticed his coming, we are not shamed but invigorated. For the first time, we look in the mirror, we go out in the world fearlessly, with a lilt in our step and a song in our heart, sensing our true worth—and the worth of all other people as well. Some children see him. Some children's souls feel their worth. All children are of immense worth. Perhaps our task is to ensure that all children see him, that all souls feel their worth.

His Law Is Love

*R*oman law was a wonder to behold. A complex, brilliantly organized legal system guaranteed a steady flow of funds into Rome's coffers. The empire rarely suffered civil strife or crime. Caesar Augustus boasted of the "peace" he brought to the world—admittedly at the end of a sharp sword and enforced by legions of armed soldiers. Augustus's law was force.

We don't think of Christmas music as revolutionary. But ponder what we hear in the second stanza of "O Holy Night": "Truly he taught us to love one another. His law is love." Law and love are totally different from each other. Law is something we must do; we have no choice. The consequences are dire if we violate the law. Love has no *must* about it. Love happens or it doesn't; it's unenforceable. Love is personal, emotional, rewarding but risky. Law is chilly, impersonal, reliable but no fun.

What Jesus taught us about love is not what the world teaches: Love is not a mood that flares and subsides but a commitment we make even to people nobody else will go near, to our enemies, to the ones who have hurt us. When Jesus was an adult, someone asked him to rank the number one law. He picked two, and both were about love: "Love the Lord your God," and "Love your neighbor" (Matt. 22:37, 39). Can love be commanded? It has been and is, at least by Jesus. "I give you a new commandment, that you love one another" (John 13:34). If Jesus commands love, we must be capable of it. But like any skill, we need practice. We do not just know how to love. We learn to love just the way we learn Spanish, or how to sew, or how to swing a golf club, or how to stick it out in a tough relationship.

Of course laws are broken, and love breaks hearts. What we need is some radical intervention into our world, to reconfigure both law and love. Maybe that's the secret of the next line from "O Holy Night": "Chains shall he break, for the slave is our brother." I can't guess what the songwriter intended, but I imagine he had something rather dramatic in mind: metal chains smashed, prisoners set free, all kinds of bondage broken. We live in a kind of bondage to self, bondage to society's sophomoric trivialization of love, bondage to a pointless life, not to mention the prevalence of real, physical oppression and injustice. Jesus became a servant (the same Greek word as *slave*), and so joined his divine self to our enslaved selves. He became our brother so we might become members of his royal family, touching off an insurrection against the unjust, bogus royalty that has usurped God's rightful place.

On the holy night Christ was born, he came to teach us to love, to show us love in the flesh, to set us free, to pioneer the path for us to become the people God wants us to be. We were made by love; we were made for love. It's commanded, and the one who commands is the one who enables, encourages, and empowers us to love God, to love one another, to love ourselves, and to put an end to oppression and injustice.

Rudolph, the Red-Nosed Reindeer

Learning God's law of love or shunning it and abiding by Caesar's law begins in childhood. At the heart of some simple childlike songs, we find a profound expression of what's gone wrong with our world—between people who should be friends or family, and even among the nations. Think of Rudolph, the Red-Nosed Reindeer, and the way the others laughed at him and called him bad names. Reindeer, like other species that are hunted, form little groups of insiders that shun the weak. And so the insiders survive, and the weak ones do not.

Who gets shoved out? The one with a red nose, darker skin color, strange accent, or different physical appearance. In every species, somebody gets mocked. Children cluster into cliques to unleash their jabs, and we scold them. But we adults never cease to snicker and call names, even if we do it in the privacy of our own narrow minds. Worst of all, at times we deceive ourselves and attach moral zeal to our abhorrence of somebody. Thankfully God did not sneer at us from the heavenly moral high ground, but God came down to love and dare to transform even the self-righteous.

One of those early Gospels that didn't make it into the Bible, "The Infancy Gospel of Thomas," regales us with a far-fetched story that I'm fond of: when Jesus was a little boy, a playmate poked fun him; he laughed and called him names. Very childishly, Jesus waved a finger and struck the boy dead; then, feeling holy remorse, he raised the boy back to life.

I bet Jesus was made fun of by other kids; surely he felt the angst, awkwardness, and shame I felt, and maybe you felt, as a child. If I'd had divine power, I would have struck down those who bullied me. On second thought, I would have cast some spell and made them play with me and pick me first for kickball. Maybe I would have made them love me. Rudolf, of course, saves the day with his red, shiny nose. The message of Christmas is even better. God doesn't say, "Hey, you've got some special ability, so you're in!" Rather, God says, "I came to form a club, and you're in before you applied or even heard of the club. There are no exclusions." The doors aren't open, because there aren't any doors. Jesus was born in an open-air manger. Jesus was just like you, whoever you are, with skin, bones, unable to say a word, crying in the night. Now we can laugh, not at anyone, but over the birth of a child—all children, actually.

DAY 5

With the Dawn
of Redeeming Grace

During Advent, we stand in the dark, eyes straining toward the horizon, eager for the coming of the Lord, the Light of the world. When this Lord arrives, what will happen? Think about what so many of us sing with candles lit in a darkened sanctuary on Christmas Eve: "Silent night, holy night . . . with the dawn of redeeming grace." The word *dawn* is alluring. Yes, it means that moment when the sun rises, though it's not really a moment at all. Dawn is a lingering stretch of moments. At first we see only darkness except for a scattering of starlight. Then near the eastern horizon the faintest glimmer, slowly but surely advancing, brighter now, clouds beginning to dazzle us with haunting then brilliant hues—and finally, the first peek of direct sunlight. Night is over; morning has broken. Oh wait, it's dawn up here but not so down in the valley. For them, the dawn is yet to come, still on its way, certain to come.

Maybe redeeming grace is just like that: It doesn't swarm in and overwhelm all at once or dawn on everyone in precisely the same way. You begin in the dark; maybe you shiver a little and wonder if there will be any redeeming grace. But you watch, wait, and continue to look for the faintest trace of grace—and then, and only then, it comes. "Weeping may linger for the night, but joy comes with the morning" (Ps. 30:5).

We also use the word *dawn* in an extended sense. "Finally it *dawned* on me what was going on!" The truth is staring you in the face, and even though you're looking right at it, you just don't get it. You have yet to connect the dots. Then, a bit more suddenly than the rising of the sun, the proverbial lightbulb pops on in your head. *How'd I miss that?* you wonder. Probably the brain process is more gradual, but the sensation is sudden. A nanosecond ago you were clueless, but now—now!—you understand.

We live in a world where Santa seems more plausible than Jesus. Santa makes and checks his list; he knows who's naughty and who's nice. We presume we'll land on the "nice" side of the ledger. We naively imagine we have some control. If I just do this and that, I'll have a jolly Christmas and a fantastic life. Perhaps once we've sat in the darkness of life for a while, it *dawns* on us: It's grace, it's mercy, it's not being naughty or nice, but it's God's love, God's stunning, unsolicited, undeserved, mind-boggling resolve to be close to me, to give me life, to redeem my hollow, pointless existence, to redeem the long list of boneheaded mistakes and wrong turns I've taken, and to give me a future not of my own devising but a pure gift from the God who holds the future securely in holy, tender hands. One Christmas back in the sixteenth century, Fra Giovanni wrote, "The gloom of the world is but a shadow. Behind it, yet within our reach, is joy. . . . There is a radiance and glory in the darkness, could we but see, and to see we have only to look. I beseech you to look!"

The grace that dawns is "redeeming." Some pious people might think redemption is the same as being saved, getting into heaven, Jesus paying for our sins. But the Bible presents a more practical way of redeeming. Your farm is in foreclosure, and you have nowhere to turn; then a rich relative you barely know plunks down some money, and you can keep working the farm and survive. You lose what is most precious to you, it's gone; then mysteriously it is bought back, and you have it again. Think through what you've lost that really mattered. At God's good dawn, when the Lord comes, all will be restored; you will make it, you'll be giddy beyond all measure.

The Bells on Christmas Day

What we've all lost, and it's so far gone we have developed a crusty acceptance of its absence, is peace. When I was a boy, I was enthralled by the Simon & Garfunkel recording of "7 O'Clock News/Silent Night," the gentle carol dubbed over by the awful news of the day. The dissonance is chilling. We shudder, and can't stop crying, when we hear the news. During Advent of 2012, twenty schoolchildren were shot to death at school in Newtown, Connecticut. If no other awful thing ever had happened in the month of December in all of history, the loss of Charlotte, Daniel, Olivia, Josephine, Ana, Dylan, Madeleine, Catherine,

Chase, Jesse, James, Grace, Emilie, Jack, Noah, Caroline, Jessica, Avielle, Benjamin, and Allison just days before Christmas would be more than enough for us to shiver and wonder why we sing "Peace on earth, good will to men." Flip through television channels. We have as much a taste for violence as we have for Christmas mirth. No wonder Henry Wadsworth Longfellow, when he "heard the bells on Christmas day," bowed his head in despair and said,

> "There is no peace on earth . . .
> > For hate is strong
> > And mocks the song
> Of peace on earth, good-will to men!"

He knew. The Civil War was raging; he'd lost two wives and a son. But with stunning resolve, with God's very Spirit streaming through his soul, he fought back the rage and cynicism—and what did he hear?

> Then pealed the bells more loud and deep:
> "God is not dead, nor doth He sleep;
> > The Wrong shall fail,
> > The Right prevail
> With peace on earth, good-will to men."

In Bethlehem, the redemptive peace that is God's will for the universe dawned. It's still shadowy down in the valley, but the sunrise is coming. The morning news is appalling, but God is not done yet. The Lord is coming. The wrong really will fail. What we read from Isaiah 9 and 11 will come to pass: "The people who walked in darkness have seen a great light. . . . For a child has been born for us," (Isa. 9:2, 6) and he is the Prince of Peace who promises us that "the wolf shall live with the lamb. . . . They shall not hurt or destroy on all my holy mountain" (Isa. 11:6, 9). Or as our carols tell us, the day foretold will dawn "when peace shall over all the earth its ancient splendors fling," and we shall "sleep in heavenly peace" every night in God's eternity.

DAY 6

Angels Bending Near the Earth

$\mathcal{S}$uddenly there was with the angel a multitude of the heavenly host, praising God and saying, 'Glory to God in the highest!'" (Luke 2:13-14). The coming of the Lord prods even the least musical among us to sing. We even sing in a foreign language! During Advent and Christmas, we hear more than our usual share of Latin being sung, and we join in ourselves: "Gloria in excelsis Deo!" Only a few of us ever studied Latin; a smattering of attorneys and biologists occasionally use a Latin term. And yet we sing in an ancient tongue in brief but meaningful solidarity with Christians from antiquity. It elevates my soul, as if God might be honored by the occasional effort to speak something grander than mere everyday English.

Sometimes church choirs sing in Latin. Should we worry if we don't understand the words? I think of the moment in *The Shawshank Redemption* when Red heard two sopranos singing from "Marriage of Figaro" over the loudspeaker in the prison yard.

I have no idea to this day what them two Italian ladies were singin' about. Truth is, I don't want to know. Some things are best left unsaid. I like to think they were singin' about something so beautiful it can't be expressed in words, and makes your heart ache because of it. I tell you, those voices soared. Higher and farther than anybody in a gray place dares to dream. It was like some beautiful bird flapped into our drab little cage and made these walls dissolve away . . . and for the briefest of moments every last man in Shawshank felt free.

The Lord's coming truly is too beautiful for words. Ours, while we dwell in this gray place, is to let our jaws drop in awe and discover that elusive feeling of freedom.

Sing All Ye Citizens of Heaven Above

We may need some help feeling awestruck and free, and God provides some hidden but certain help. At Christmas we sing to one another, "O come let us adore him," but it's the third stanza of that great carol that surprises us: "Sing, choirs of angels . . . sing, all ye citizens of heaven above!"

Outsiders to the faith, skeptics of things spiritual, would consider us lunatics. But we believe in the communion of the saints, that the dead, and the angels of heaven, undergird our singing, provide hidden harmonies, and launch into descants in a pitch so marvelous that only those who have adored the "Word of the Father, now in flesh appearing" even notice. When we sing, we might just detect the subtle presence of those first shepherds, the faithful through the centuries, saints and martyrs, even kinfolk we've loved and lost, a host of angels and disciples joining in our song. We do not sing alone, and a holy host far more numerous than we can physically count in our sanctuaries sing along to each carol.

To Touch Their Harps of Gold

Luke 2:14 tells us the heavenly host said, "Peace on earth." We in turn sing of what "came upon a midnight clear"—"that glorious song of old . . . Peace on earth." We may sing of peace, but we've forgotten how to dream of peace or how to work for it. We've become hard and cynical; we've adjusted to a failure of peace out in the world, in our homes, and in our own hearts. When Jesus was born, the angels sang "peace on earth"—and they weren't just teasing. Peace is very real with God. Can we trust the song? Can we sing and pray for peace, insist upon peace, expect peace, and have no peace until there is peace?

Angels are "bending near the earth, to touch their harps of gold," far below heaven, ever closer to the ground, playing the song of God's love, mercy, justice and power, the melody of peace, the harmony of God's kingdom dawning. How long before we hear? "For lo! the days are hastening on." Perhaps we are incapable of peace—but God is able.

Wondrous Star, Lend Thy Light

The most beautiful moment of every year for me is at the end of our Christmas Eve service when we lower the artificial lights and raise small candles as we sing "Silent Night." As the pastor standing up front, I enjoy the best view of the little planetarium we create in God's house, heaven in miniature, a constellation of longing, a galaxy of hope. Inevitably I tremble a bit when I see it.

The light is in our very own hands! I could raise a single candle in front of everyone, and it might be quaint; but together we raise our candles—the newlyweds, teens and retirees, the depressed and the unemployed, the grieving and the giddy, the one who's never been to church much, and the one who is unwittingly singing "Silent Night" for his very last time.

As we lift our candles, we sing, "Wondrous star, lend thy light." Dante spoke of "the love that moves the sun and the other stars," and we believe it was love that caused the stars to exist. Love fashioned the earth as the perfect theater for God to show off, to display what kind of God we're dealing with. "In the beginning was the Word. . . . All things came into being through him. . . . The light shines in the darkness, and the darkness did not overcome it" (John 1:1-5). Our God is no remote Olympian deity. Our God looks for all the world like a young child, holding a small candle, her small voice echoing "with the angels, let us sing." God's light is not a massive torch or a wildfire out of control. God's light is small, just a flicker. A child can handle it! Even a small candle can banish the darkness, and we see the beauty of God in the face of a child.

"Wondrous star, lend thy light." Don't give it to me to keep, Lord. It's on loan, just for a time. Our chief delight isn't to soak up this light but to reflect it, to be a mirror of the starry wonder to others. The "radiant beams from thy holy face" transfix us, and we then do some radiant beaming to others who could use the lending of some light themselves. And the candlelight is over far too quickly—like our brief lives on this earth. So we do not postpone joy or procrastinate in getting connected to the Christ child or tarry in beaming that light to others. In the moment, this moment, we go ahead and sing "Alleluia to our King!—and "all is bright." It really is "the dawn of redeeming grace."

Leader's Guide

$\mathcal{W}$elcome to the leader's guide for *Why This Jubilee?* Each session includes an opening prayer, a Christmas carol, a series of conversation starters, a closing prayer, and a preview question for the next week. Light a candle on an Advent wreath each week to celebrate the season.

Please don't feel compelled to get through every conversation starter offered each week! Pick and choose based on your group and what gets people talking.

The study will work best if people read the assigned book sections before each gathering. Make sure participants have a copy of the book. The sessions can stand alone, and a participant can miss a week without a problem.

There are a few materials listed in the guide for each session. Bring hymnals or the words to the Christmas carols you will sing each week for each participant.

Why This Jubilee? offers readers a chance to explore the Advent season in a meaningful way. May God bless this rich experience for you!

WEEK 1: *The Place*

Materials

Whiteboard and markers, hymnals or copies of "O Little Town of Bethlehem," Advent wreath

Opening Prayer

Light one candle on the Advent wreath.

Jesus, you know everything about us by heart. You love the carols in each of us. And we love to sing about you. May we sing your songs and hear your Word as we await your coming. Amen.

Hymn

"O Little Town of Bethlehem"

Conversation Starters

"Silence is God's language" (15). How is God's Advent language of silence distinctly different from the sound of Christmas preparations? Where do you go to find silence during this season? Does silence appeal to you?

"Our Christmas lists will seem trivial compared to the riches God wants for us. God's job isn't to grant our big wishes. God shows us something higher, far beyond what we could wish for on our own" (25). Make two lists on a whiteboard with these questions: *What do we want for Christmas?* and *What does God want for each of us and for our community this Christmas?* Compare the lists.

"Mary and Joseph went for a long ride together. . . . [They] probably sang to stiffen their courage and bolster their spirits" (28). What are your favorite seasonal songs? What does Psalm 96:1, 10-11, 13 teach us about how to observe Advent?

"The Hebrew, *beth-lehem*, means 'House of Bread.' . . . Can you grow spiritually in food giving from one Advent to the next?" (34). What are your baking and giving traditions during Advent? How have you been encouraged to change your giving habits this Advent?

"'The hopes and fears of all the years are met in thee tonight.' . . . Hope and fear seem to be antithetical, as if they emerge from opposite ends of the soul" (35). What are your hopes and fears for the world this Advent? How are our hopes and fears intertwined with those of your neighbors and with Jesus' love?

Howell focuses on place during this first week of Advent. What Christmas places do you remember from childhood?

Closing Prayer

O holy Child of Bethlehem, descend to us, we pray;
Cast out our sin, and enter in, be born in us today.

(Pause to invite participants to add their joys and concerns)

We hear the Christmas angels the great glad tidings tell;
O, come to us, abide with us, our Lord Emmanuel! Amen.

For Next Week

Read *Week 2: The Men* for the next meeting. Here is something to ponder until next time: "We think the powers do what they do because they are all-powerful. But God uses even the high and mighty, unbeknownst to them, to achieve God's purposes" (52). Name and pray for several world leaders who might find themselves surprising vessels of God's justice and grace.

WEEK 2: *The Men*

Materials

Hymnals or copies of "Angels We Have Heard on High," Advent wreath

Opening Prayer

Light two candles on the Advent wreath.

Jesus, you know everything about us by heart. You love the carols in each of us. And we love to sing about you. May we sing your songs and hear your Word as we await your coming. Amen.

Hymn

"Angels We Have Heard on High"

Conversation Starters

"Theologically, Advent has been conceived as a season of repentance" (43). How do you feel each year when John the Baptist shows up at the beginning of Advent with a message of repentance? From what do you need to detach yourself in order to celebrate Christmas the way God wants you to this year?

"Joseph can help us. Confronted by the scandalous surprise of God becoming flesh, granting every good reason to flee for the exits and be the center of attention in our own dramas, maybe this Advent we can learn what it means just to stand near the manger, to look, to wait, to stay, to trust" (49).

What examples of Joseph's faith and endurance do you see in those around you? How does being a parent, aunt, uncle, or mentor teach us to look, wait, stay, and trust like Joseph?

"We think the powers do what they do because they are all-powerful. But God uses even the high and mighty, unbeknownst to them, to achieve God's purposes" (52). Name and pray for several world leaders who might find themselves surprising vessels of God's justice and grace.

"But the shepherds stood before Jesus in awe, the way we crowd around a crib holding a sleeping child" (57). Have you ever considered yourself to be like a shepherd when you've watched a sleeping baby? Who are the babies or children in your life this Advent? What have they taught you about God's love?

"God gives us much that is far better than our deepest desiring. God gives God's own self" (63). What is the best gift you've ever received? What is the best gift you've ever given? How could you give of yourself this year?

"And we may chuckle or shrink back a little over Elie Wiesel's clever remark: 'Whenever an angel says, "Be not afraid!" you'd better start worrying. A big assignment is on the way'" (66). How do God's assignments differ from your to-do list? When has an angel told you not to be afraid?

Closing Prayer

Shepherds, why this jubilee? Why your joyous strains prolong?
Say what may the tidings be which inspire your heav'nly song?

(Pause to invite participants to add their joys and concerns)

Come to Bethlehem and see Christ whose birth the angels sing;
Come adore on bended knee Christ, the Lord, the newborn King.

For Next Week

Read *Week 3: The Mother* for the next meeting. Here is something to ponder until next time: "Jesus learned the wonder of mothering from Mary. And the pledge to us all, especially during the Advent season when we feel the pangs of family dysfunction or grieve the loss of mothers and others loved ones, is that Jesus can be mother, sister, brother, and father to us who need family, grace, and belonging at the deepest core of our beings" (96). What parts of your life could use Jesus' mothering?

WEEK 3: *The Mother*

Materials

Hymnals or copies of "What Child Is This," Advent wreath

Opening Prayer

Light three candles on the Advent wreath.

Jesus, you know everything about us by heart. You love the carols in each of us. And we love to sing about you. May we sing your songs and hear your Word as we await your coming. Amen.

Hymn

"What Child Is This"

Conversation Starters

"God chooses the unlikely. God assigns undoable tasks. God seems utterly uninterested in ability. What God wants is availability. During Advent, ask yourself, *Am I available for the coming of the Lord and whatever might be asked of me?*" (71). Look at your phone calendar, text messages, or e-mail right now. If God said, "Clear all that and follow me," what would you do next?

"Martin Luther called the Bible 'the swaddling clothes in which Jesus is laid.' To get near Mary and her son Jesus, to think their thoughts and love what they loved, we immerse ourselves in the scripture's stories, songs, laws, and prayers" (74). When you open your Bible this Advent, what stories are you looking for?

What stories might be looking for you? To whom could you give a Bible for Christmas this year?

"A mother's cradling of new life is the clearest possible window into God's heart. God thought, *I want them to know me—so I will do this. I will be born and tenderly embraced by my mother, just like all of them*" (78). Imagine how a mother in the developing world whose new baby may not survive for lack of food or clean water hears the Christmas story.

"God does things we couldn't dream of achieving" (89). What do you wish God could achieve this Christmas that is completely beyond your power to enact?

"Jesus learned the wonder of mothering from Mary. And the pledge to us all, especially during the Advent season when we feel the pangs of family dysfunction or grieve the loss of mothers and others loved ones, is that Jesus can be mother, sister, brother, and father to us who need family, grace, and belonging at the deepest core of our beings" (96). What parts of your life could use Jesus' mothering?

Closing Prayer

What Child is this, who laid to rest, on Mary's lap is sleeping?
Whom angels greet with anthems sweet, while shepherds watch are keeping?

(Pause to invite participants to add their joys and concerns)

This, this is Christ, the King, whom shepherds guard and angels sing;
Haste, haste to bring him laud, the Babe, the Son of Mary. Amen.

For Next Week

Read *Week 4: The Child* for the next meeting. Here is something to ponder until next time: "God comes to us where we are, as we are, not merely to bless us but to leave us forever changed. God comes to transform us, to take us somewhere" (109). Where would you be afraid for God to take you this Advent? What keeps you from saying yes to God's transformation?

WEEK 4: *The Child*

Materials

Hymnals or copies of "Away in a Manger," Advent wreath, a Christmas card and writing utensil for each participant

Opening Prayer

Light four candles on the Advent wreath.

Jesus, you know everything about us by heart. You love the carols in each of us. And we love to sing about you. May we sing your songs and hear your Word as we await your coming. Amen.

Hymn

"Away in a Manger"

Conversation Starters

"Jesus showed us the heart of God most spectacularly—as a humble nobody, sleeping in the most ignoble quarters, consorting with questionable people, laying down his life, bearing shame, and abandoning all privilege" (100). How would you describe the heart of God to a nonbeliever, to a teenager, to someone who slept outside last night? What might each of them want to know about the heart of God?

"God became like us: We cry, so Jesus cried" (106). What carols, sights, stories, and feelings of the Advent season bring you to tears? How are your tears connected to Jesus' tears and the cries of God's people?

"God comes to us where we are, as we are, not merely to bless us but to leave us forever changed. God comes to transform us, to take us somewhere" (109). Where would you be afraid for God to take you this Advent? What keeps you from saying yes to God's transformation?

"We were made by love; we were made for love. It's commanded, and the one who commands is the one who enables, encourages, and empowers us to love God, to love one another, to love ourselves, and to put an end to oppression and injustice" (112–3). What hard-to-love person would God like each of us to love this Christmas? Take some time to write that person a Christmas card. Take the card home, put it in your Bible, and talk to God about what to do next.

"God's light is small, just a flicker. A child can handle it! Even a small candle can banish the darkness, and we see the beauty of God in the face of a child" (124). What has enlightened you this Advent? What do children help you to believe about Jesus?

What do you think you will remember throughout the coming year from this Advent small group? What was your favorite section of *Why This Jubilee*?

Closing Prayer

Be near me, Lord Jesus, I ask thee to stay
Close by me forever, and love me, I pray;

(Pause to invite participants to add their joys and concerns)

Bless all the dear children in thy tender care,
And fit us for heaven to live with thee there. Amen.

Notes

1. Frederick Buechner, *Secrets in the Dark: A Life in Sermons* (New York: HarperCollins, 2006), 11.
2. Charles Dickens, *A Christmas Carol & Other Christmas Stories* (New York: Penguin, 1984), 35.
3. Martin Luther King, Jr., *A Testament of Hope: The Essential Writings of Martin Luther King Jr.*, ed. James M. Washington (San Francisco: Harper & Row, 1986), 282.
4. James H. Forest, *Love Is the Measure: A Biography of Dorothy Day* (Maryknoll, NY: Orbis Books, 1986), 135.
5. Taylor Branch, *Parting the Waters: America in the King Years 1954-63* (New York: Simon & Schuster, 1988), 99.
6. Robert McAfee Brown, *Spirituality and Liberation: Overcoming the Great Fallacy* (Louisville, KY: Westminster John Knox Press, 1988), 136.
7. Madeleine L'Engle, *A Cry Like a Bell* (Wheaton, IL: Harold Shaw Publishers, 2000), 55.
8. Carlo Carretto, *Blessed Are You Who Believed*, trans. Barbara Wall (Tunbridge Wells, UK: Burns & Oates, 1982), 75.
9. *Mother Teresa*, directed by Ann and Jeanette Petrie (San Francisco: Petrie Productions, 1986), DVD.
10. Julian of Norwich, *Showings: Classics of Western Spirituality*, trans. and ed. Edmund Colledge and James Walsh (Mahwah, NJ: Paulist Press, 1978), 295, 297, 301.
11. C. S. Lewis, *The Weight of Glory: And Other Addresses*, ed. Walter Hooper (New York: HarperCollins, 1980), 26.

CPSIA information can be obtained
at www.ICGtesting.com
Printed in the USA
LVHW082052101122
732859LV00010B/430

9 780835 814959